Managing AI Wisely

NEW HORIZONS IN BUSINESS ANALYTICS

Series Editor: *Richard Vidgen*, Professor of Business Analytics, UNSW Business School, Australia and Emeritus Professor of Systems Thinking, University of Hull, UK

We are proud to present a new series of ground-breaking short books defining the future of research in business analytics, edited by Professor Richard Vidgen.

Giving a concise 'must-read, must-cite' take, the books will be more in depth than a journal article, shorter than a standard book and stimulating to read, giving authors the freedom to expand on their research.

The series will cover topics such as algorithmic decision-making, artificial intelligence and data-driven management in different organizational contexts, as well as exploring important themes such as sustainability and ethics. To this end, the series intends to further our understanding of the full potential and pitfalls of analytics in business and management.

Academically rigorous while maintaining relevance in practice, these books are intended to be an excellent starting point to explore new avenues of research for new and established academics.

Managing AI Wisely
From Development to Organizational Change in Practice

Lauren Waardenburg

Assistant Professor of Management Information Systems, IESEG School of Management, France

Marleen Huysman

Professor of Knowledge and Organization, KIN Center for Digital Innovation, Vrije Universiteit Amsterdam, the Netherlands

Marlous Agterberg

Research and Valorization Manager, KIN Center for Digital Innovation, Vrije Universiteit Amsterdam, the Netherlands

NEW HORIZONS IN BUSINESS ANALYTICS

Edward Elgar
PUBLISHING

Cheltenham, UK • Northampton, MA, USA

First published in Dutch as *S.L.I.M. managen van AI in de praktijk* by Stichting Management Studies (SMS), 2020. Translated by Vertaalbureau Textwerk.

Published by
Edward Elgar Publishing Limited
The Lypiatts
15 Lansdown Road
Cheltenham
Glos GL50 2JA
UK

Edward Elgar Publishing, Inc.
William Pratt House
9 Dewey Court
Northampton
Massachusetts 01060
USA

A catalogue record for this book
is available from the British Library

Library of Congress Control Number: 2021944938

This book is available electronically in the **Elgar**online
Business subject collection
http://dx.doi.org/10.4337/9781800887671

ISBN 978 1 80088 766 4 (cased)
ISBN 978 1 80088 767 1 (eBook)

Printed and bound by CPI Group (UK) Ltd, Croydon, CR0 4YY

Contents

Figures

Tables

Boxes

About the authors

Dr. Marlous Agterberg is Research and Valorization Manager at the KIN Center for Digital Innovation, Vrije Universiteit Amsterdam, the Netherlands. After having worked as researcher for ten years, she is in her current position responsible for creating social impact with the top academic research that is executed at KIN. She sets up new research collaborations with organizations and strives to bring academia and business closer together.

Marleen Huysman is Professor of Knowledge and Organizations and the Director of the KIN Center for Digital Innovation, Vrije Universiteit Amsterdam, the Netherlands. Her research relates to the development and use of digital technology in practice and has been published in international top-tier academic journals and books. She is a frequent academic and professional speaker. Marleen is author of the book *Sharing Knowledge in Practice*.

Lauren Waardenburg is Assistant Professor of Management Information Systems at IESEG School of Management, Lille, France. She conducted her PhD at the KIN Center for Digital Innovation. Her research is focused on how algorithmic technologies are changing the future of work. She conducted ethnographic research across a period of three years into the use of AI in the Dutch Police Force.

Acknowledgements

First of all, we would like to express our gratitude to our colleagues at the KIN Center for Digital Innovation who stimulated us and helped to write the book. We would like to specifically acknowledge Elmira van den Broek, Bomi Kim, Ella Hafermalz, Mario Sosa Hidalgo, Maura Soekijad, Çiğdem Yıldız Uzun and Claudia Egher for their help with the data collection and the effort they have put into the case descriptions.

We are immensely grateful to the case organizations, and all employees involved, who opened their doors to us. This book would not have existed without your enthusiasm and cooperation.

We thank Jochem Hummel for his critical eye on the completion of the manuscript.

Finally, we are grateful to Stichting Management Studies for the opportunity to write this book. We would like to thank especially Nicolaas Weeda and Chandni Sital. We thank our supervisory committee – Jules van der Perre, Anne Megens, Dick Okhuijsen, Guido Heezen, Merijn Zee, Robin Spierings and Roelof Meijer – for their commitment and involvement in the development of this book.

Summary

Artificial intelligence (AI) refers to a field in computer science that focuses on developing systems that can accomplish tasks that normally require human intelligence. AI uses, among other things, machine learning (self-learning) algorithms, which can learn based on large amounts of data. As a result, an AI system can independently come up with new suggestions, decisions or predictions.

This book is about managing AI systems in practice. As far as we are concerned, the word 'practice' should be emphasized, because although there are many (popular) scientific publications about the potential influence of AI systems on work and organizations, little of this work is based on real cases that can provide examples from practice. This is specifically important because existing literature on technology and work suggest that a gap may exist between the development of technology and its actual use in daily work, which might trigger unforeseen consequences. It is time to explore what these consequences are.

In this book, we provide insight into the implementation and use of AI in organizations, without losing sight of the development of the technology. To this end, we conducted research at eight incumbent organizations that have introduced AI systems into their existing work processes. From our analysis of the conversations and observations we conducted, and the written information about the organizations, we have identified four themes that specifically apply to the management of AI systems:

1. Organizing for data. To gather or create data – the central building block of AI – management activities that focus on organizing for data are required.
2. Testing and validating. Since AI systems can automate tasks that were previously undertaken by humans, AI systems can potentially have major consequences for people, organizations and society. Due to the black-boxed nature of AI systems, testing and validating AI systems is becoming increasingly complex. Consequently, the question of whether and when AI systems are good enough is not merely technical, but certainly also a management issue.
3. Algorithmic brokering. The black-boxed character also affects the applicability of the AI results. Often, these results still have to be interpreted

and/or translated before they can be used, which is difficult due to its black-boxed characteristic. More and more organizations are choosing to create a role for a so-called algorithmic broker to deal with this unexplainability.

4. Changes to work. The self-learning aspect of AI also provides new knowledge. That is why AI, unlike prior technologies, is focused on knowledge work. When you implement new knowledge in an organization, where knowledge is often implicit and distributed across different groups of actors, there is a good chance that this will cause (unexpected) changes to work.

The four themes stem from three unique characteristics of AI: (1) it relies on large amounts of data; (2) it is self-learning and difficult to explain, that is, how outputs are generated is 'black-boxed'; and (3) it is focused on knowledge work. This makes AI a fundamentally different technology compared to what organizations have previously been confronted with. It therefore requires new forms of management. To manage AI systems successfully in practice, we offer four 'WISE' recommendations. Wisely managing AI systems requires:

- Work-related insights. AI systems should be based on work-related insights concerning data, testing and validation, algorithmic brokering and changes to work.
- Interdisciplinary knowledge. Different disciplines (developers, users, managers) should be brought together and, where necessary, additional training should be provided.
- Sociotechnical change processes. The introduction of AI should be seen as an organizational change process and, conversely, the technology should be tailored to the needs of the work processes.
- Ethical awareness. Discussions should take place regarding ethical considerations and the explainability of AI systems and their underlying assumptions.

In this book, we require a lot of responsibility from the manager. We are convinced that managers, as important decision-makers in the organization, have a central role and responsibility in implementing and managing AI systems. However, we do not imply that the described responsibilities can or should be performed by a single manager. A wise manager creates a wise team to wisely introduce and manage AI.

AI systems can offer organizations numerous opportunities and can fundamentally transform work for the better. We hope this book will convince managers to look beyond the 'AI hype' and keep asking themselves, at all times, irrespective of which stage they are at: 'Are we managing AI wisely?'

1.   Introduction to managing AI wisely

1.1   PREFACE

Artificial intelligence (AI) refers to a field in computer science concerned with creating systems that can accomplish tasks that normally require human intelligence (Nilsson, 1971; Pesapane et al., 2018). AI systems use machine learning (self-learning) algorithms, which can learn using large amounts of data. As a result, an AI system can independently come up with, for example, new suggestions, decisions or predictions.

Our interest in the influence of AI systems on work and organizations dates back to the time when organizations hardly talked about AI, and the systems that were implemented were not yet self-learning. During that time, between 2012 and 2014, one of the then PhD students of our research group studied the implementation of data analytics in the sales process of a large telecom organization. The organization had enthusiastically switched to so-called customer lifecycle management (CLM), in short, determining performance by measuring customer statistics. This data analytics initiative would provide a new and more efficient way of working in the sales department where, at that time, account managers were still responsible for customer relations. However, what actually happened was of a completely different order. It soon became apparent that the developers of the analytics system had a different idea of what work at the sales department entailed compared to the account managers themselves. For example, the developers were convinced that their model would help account managers to approach 'the right customer, at the right time, with the right offer' out of 300 customers per manager. The account managers, on the other hand, were convinced that 'such a data-based model' could never reflect the information they obtained by 'actually talking to the customer'. The account managers had built up relational knowledge (based on the relationship with customers); for example, they memorized the names of the customer's children, which the CLM system did not record.

Nevertheless, the organization continued to implement CLM and the account managers were asked to register each time they used a CLM suggestion to make their customer contact. In practice, the account managers hardly ever used CLM, but they felt that this was expected of them by management. To meet leadership expectations, the account managers deliberately indicated after each customer contact that this was based on a CLM suggestion. Although almost all customer contacts remained based on the relational knowledge of the account managers, the 'fake' registrations made it seem that CLM was almost always right. This ultimately backfired for the account managers, for management decided that half of the account managers could be fired. After all, the CLM system was almost always right, which indicated that a lot less time needed to be spent building and maintaining customer relationships. When half of the account managers left the sales department, chaos ensued. Only after their departure did it become obvious that the important relational knowledge had been lost. In the end, it emerged that CLM was by no means such a 'holy grail' as was initially thought, but by then it was too late (Pachidi et al., 2021).

This was 2014, and CLM was but a relatively simple analytics system. Although some would argue that they were already dealing with an 'intelligent algorithm' (IA), it was by no means an 'intelligent system' like self-learning algorithms. This example shows, however, the potential dangers and implications that increasingly advanced, data-driven technologies can have for work and expertise. In the meantime, technological developments have not stood still, and increasingly complex self-learning algorithms are being implemented in organizations. Organizations have become increasingly confident in the possibilities of AI systems, and more and more organizations are now truly entering the field of AI.

The technological developments of recent years have meant that in our work we increasingly have to deal with AI systems that, by learning from large amounts of data, can perform tasks that were previously the purview of people. For example, they can provide legal support by digging through lengthy documents in seconds (Zhang et al., 2020) and pinpointing where specific information can be found, and they can help doctors to detect tumours that are sometimes invisible to the human eye (Kim et al., 2021). Even now, it is assumed that no technology since the start of the digital revolution some 60 years ago will have so many consequences for work and organizations. The unparalleled growth in data and technological knowledge assures that these consequences will likely only increase in the coming years.

In this book, we describe the opportunities and possibilities that the implementation of AI systems offers to organizations, while also considering the associated risks. The above example shows the danger of losing valuable knowledge based on an unsubstantiated belief in a new technology. This risk rises with the implementation of increasingly advanced AI systems. In addition, AI systems are unique because they simulate knowledge work. As an important characteristic of knowledge work is that it depends on collaboration between experts, when an AI system is implemented in a specific part of the organization, it is likely to have unexpected consequences beyond its intended effect. This can lead to negative results for organizations if such 'ripple effects' are not taken into account (Baptista et al., 2020). Another important character-istic of AI systems is the self-learning characteristic which makes the systems difficult to understand (also called 'black-boxed'). Fewer and fewer people are able to explain what goes on within an AI system, or the logic that suggestions or predictions are based on. This can have a major influence on who has a say in the implementation and use of AI systems.

Based on eight incumbent European organizations that introduced AI systems into their existing work processes, we describe how to deal with chal-lenges of managing AI in practice. In our research, we encountered four main themes: organizing for data, testing and validating, algorithmic brokers and changing work. These four themes are interrelated (see Figure 1.1) and form the core chapters of this book.

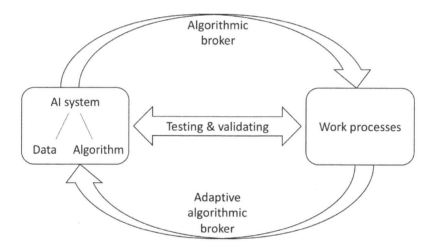

Figure 1.1   Overview of core themes

Organizing for data focuses on the management activities that are necessary to gather, construct and produce data. As the central building block of AI, data ensures that algorithms can be trained and AI systems can be developed (the left side of Figure 1.1). There is often talk of the possibilities of decontextu-alized Big Data for organizations. The cases described in this book show that internal, contextual data is of crucial importance for the development of AI systems that fit well with established work processes. The challenge for man-agement is to step beyond the 'blind spot of Big Data' to organize effectively for the construction and production of data that is of added value to AI system development.

Testing and validating refer to the need to make decisions about when and whether AI systems are 'good enough' to perform tasks (at the centre of Figure 1.1). Since AI systems can automate tasks that were previously undertaken by humans, they can potentially have major consequences for people, organizations and society. However, the black-boxed nature of AI systems makes testing and validating difficult, for it is almost impossible to find out how the results come about. The question of whether and when an AI system is good enough is therefore not only technical but also managerial. The challenge is to integrate the work processes and to test and validate against various criteria.

Algorithmic brokers refer to the fact that the outcomes of AI systems can only rarely be adopted as a 'ready-to-use product'. Instead, outcomes often have to be interpreted, filtered and translated. Here again, the black-boxed nature of AI systems makes interpreting and translating the results extremely challenging. More and more organizations are choosing to create a new role: the algorithmic broker (top of Figure 1.1). The challenge is to enable this new role to be adaptive, and to support both users and developers (bottom of Figure 1.1).

Changing work refers to a broader perspective on the consequences of the introduction of AI systems for work processes (the right side of Figure 1.1). Through the self-learning aspect of AI, it is able to generate new knowledge. When new knowledge is introduced within organizations, where knowledge is often implicit and scattered, there is a good chance that (unexpected) changes will result. The challenge is to manage the use of AI and the new knowledge in such a way that organizations are faced with as few surprises as possible, and that work is enriched through automation rather than made redundant.

1.2   BACKGROUND OF THE BOOK

Although the concept of AI has been around for almost 70 years, the attention from organizations towards intelligent systems has only in recent years increased exponentially. Of course, this is not accidental, as this relates to the widespread organizational access to the necessary computing power and the large amounts of data collected. Despite this, little is known about what managing AI looks like in practice. Gaining a thorough insight into this requires actually 'going into the field', to speak with developers, managers and users to observe first hand what is exactly happening in practice. We did this for this book, in which we were guided by three principles.

The first principle is narrowing down the term 'AI'. Although we cannot avoid it, we use the concept of AI with some caution. 'AI' is mainly used as an umbrella term indicating a field that covers a large number of technologies, methods and models. For example, with AI one can imply a simple calculation module in an Excel spreadsheet, but also a robot arm, or a forecasting system.

As a result, the concept of AI runs the risk of being too generic. In addition, the term 'AI' evokes associations with magic, mysticism and even hype, that do not contribute to understanding or taking responsibility for intelligent systems. In order to make proper use of the term 'AI', in Chapter 2 we pay attention to what we mean by AI, from a technical point of view, whereby the self-learning element of algorithms plays a central role. In addition, throughout the book we speak about 'AI systems' as the technology and 'AI' as the field in which such systems reside.

The second principle is focusing on AI systems in practice. There are different schools of thought in AI research. For example, the computer science movement mainly focuses on creating and improving algorithms and is concerned with technological optimization. Another school is concerned with the ethical issues surrounding the development of AI. However, both trends focus on the stand-alone intelligent systems. Although these streams of research hold a rich body of critical and inspiring views for both managers and scientists, the disadvantage is that such studies are hardly based on concrete examples from practice. It remains unclear whether such conceptual ideas will unfold as expected in practice. To a large extent, both the successes and the dangers of AI systems are yet to be proven in practice. Existing literature on technology and work teaches us that there can be a gap between the development of technology and its actual use in daily work, which can lead to unforeseen consequences. This book provides insight into the implementation and use of AI, without losing sight of the development of technology.

The third principle is attention to managing change. Much (mainstream) scientific work focuses on the development and the implementation of AI as two separate processes. This book deviates from this focus as it deals with managing AI as an organizational change process in which development, implementation and use are intertwined. To do this, we focus our attention on the work practices within organizations, which are not about individual tasks of employees, but about how different tasks and actors relate to each other. In addition, many of the initiatives surrounding AI are focused on the possibility of intelligent systems to change work and organizations as we know them today, for example by completely replacing work or automating large parts of work. This deterministic viewpoint espouses a view where AI systems will unilaterally transform the world as we know it in a path-dependent way. In this book, we abandon this idea and look at the relations between organization and technology, whereby the technology changes the organization, but the organization also has a significant influence on the (further) development of the technology.

Our approach makes the book particularly suitable for managers, for whom the book can function as a guide. We provide management insight into the need for an integrated approach to AI. We emphasize the complexity and

Table 1.1   Overview of cases included in the book

Organization	Industry	AI system	Stage of implementation
ABN AMRO	Finance	Anti money laundering system	Use
Centraal Beheer (CB)	Insurance	Helpdesk chatbot	Use
Dutch Police Force	Government	Predictive policing	Use
KLM	Airline	Meals-on-Board System	Use
LUMC (radiology)	Healthcare	Predictive tumour modelling	Implementation
MultiCo[a] (recruitment)	HR	Predictive people analytics	Use
Philadelphia	Healthcare	Social robotics	Implementation
Volkswagen	Automotive	Smart powerplants	Use

Note:
a. A pseudonym. The name of the organization remains anonymous for privacy reasons.

challenges, but also the opportunities that such an approach offers for the optimal development and implementation of AI in the workplace. The book's practice-oriented approach helps managers to develop their own ideas and strategy, inspired by the examples described. For this reason, we have chosen only to involve organizations that have gained concrete experience with the development and implementation of AI in existing work processes. The advantage of such an approach is that we can make well-founded statements about the success factors and challenges to managing AI in practice.

1.3   CASE SELECTION

The case examples in this book provide as broad a picture as possible of how organizations deal with managing AI in practice. At the start of our search, the doors to many organizations remained closed to us. Often, organizations feared losing their competitive advantage through cooperation, divulging confidential information, or even suffering reputational damage. Fortunately, we found eight large European organizations willing to cooperate that met our selection criteria (see also Table 1.1). We have anonymized only one of these organizations for privacy reasons. In the following sections, we discuss the case selection criteria used and associated limitations.

1.3.1   Selection Criteria

For selecting our cases, we maintained six specific criteria:

1. We have chosen to focus on incumbent organizations introducing AI into their existing work processes. Therefore, we do not examine cases where AI is at the core of the business model; tech companies (Google,

Tesla, bol.com, Booking.com, or Netflix) and startups are not part of our research. The aim of our book is to provide a realistic picture of what current managers and organizations are dealing with, or will have to deal with when introducing AI at work. While the development and use of AI by tech companies is an interesting topic deserving attention, it is beyond the scope of this book.

2. In order to guarantee consistency in the use of the term 'AI', we have set the condition that the system studied must use some form of machine learning in order to be referred to as an AI system. By focusing on machine learning algorithms, we exclude earlier, perhaps more embedded systems (such as expert systems). We do this with the intention to highlight the unique qualities that make AI systems so special and influential.

3. Because our aim is to provide insight into how to manage AI in practice, we have selected cases that have developed at least a first version of an AI system and are therefore in the implementation phase (see Table 1.1). Organizations in the implementation phase usually have less experience than organizations that have already started using AI systems. We had to drop a number of cases during the data collection process that were too early-stage and where the AI system was not yet sufficiently developed. Despite the often interesting initiatives, dropped organizations had gained too little experience in the actual management of AI.

4. We have specifically chosen to source real-world examples from as wide a range of industries as possible, including professional services, healthcare providers, finance and government.

5. Because we want to keep the culture within organizations as constant as possible in our description, we have focused on Western European organizations.

6. An important precondition was, of course, whether the organizations were willing to contribute to the realization of this book, by name or by pseudonym. Although we found several closed doors in our search for suitable cases, the organizations involved in this book enthusiastically cooperated in providing information, with only one organization wanting to be anonymized.

1.3.2 Research Limitations

This book is not about the many failed attempts at implementing AI systems (like the example of the telecom organization at the beginning of this chapter). There are plenty of organizations that believe they can gain a competitive advantage by developing an AI system based on having a lot of data, without having a clear goal for the use of these systems. We have chosen to disregard these failed attempts because our focus in this book is on the choices and challenges that managers face to successfully implement AI in the long term.

There is a lot of speculation about the specific benefits of implementing AI systems: more efficiency, innovation, objectivity, and so on. However, we cannot yet answer with a resounding 'yes' the question of whether AI actually offers added value in the organizations we have studied. While we would like to argue otherwise, AI is still in its infancy when it comes to implementation in incumbent organizations. Organizations that have already gone through the entire 'AI journey' and have entered the phase of full institutionalization are therefore scarce. We see, though, that AI is not a 'danger' for work. The cases in this book show that new tasks, functions and jobs are added that we could not have foreseen in advance.

Generalization is not our goal, and we emphasize that the choice of eight cases does not necessarily make the study representative of the management of AI in practice. Our aim in this book is to describe and analyse practical cases to provide insight into how a number of leading organizations deal with the implementation and management of AI in practice. Because organizations all approach this in their own, unique ways, we derive a number of success factors and challenges from the cases, which we trust that managers from other organizations can benefit from.

1.4   CHAPTER OVERVIEW

Following this introduction, we describe the background of AI in Chapter 2. We place AI within a historical context and describe how it evolved into a broad concept that covers many different technologies today. We also explain the techniques that are classified as AI and which criteria for AI we have used for this book. In Chapter 3, we discuss current research into AI in the workplace. We discuss existing theories and perspectives around AI and work, with which we lay the foundation for the practical, case-based chapters. In addition, we also discuss current developments regarding 'responsible AI'.

In Chapters 4 to 8, we include our cases. In Chapter 4, we first discuss the research methods used and then provide a general introduction for each case. This can be used as a reading guide in the following chapters. Using the cases in Chapters 5 to 8, we discuss the four main themes we identify as specific to managing AI in practice: organizing for data, testing and validating, algorithmic brokers, and changes to work. To keep the chapters clear, we select specific elements of cases to discuss in detail in each chapter (see Table 1.2 for an overview of the division of the cases in the chapters). In Chapter 9, we end the book with practical recommendations for adopting intelligent systems. These recommendations are brought together under the acronym WISE, which

Table 1.2   *Overview of cases per chapter*

Chapter	Section	Cases
Chapter 5 Organizing for data	5.2.1 The process of data construction	MultiCo: predictive people analytics Philadelphia: social robotics
	5.2.2 New roles for data construction	CB: helpdesk chatbot LUMC: predictive tumour modelling
	5.2.3 From data to algorithm	MultiCo: predictive people analytics
Chapter 6 Testing and validating	6.2.1 Validating using technical conditions and guidelines	KLM: consumption prediction ABN AMRO: money laundering prediction Volkswagen: smart generators
	6.2.2 Work processes as part of validation	Police: predictive policing Philadelphia: social robotics
	6.2.3 Managing expectations and trust	KLM: consumption prediction Philadelphia: social robotics
Chapter 7 Algorithmic brokers	7.2.1 Regular algorithmic brokers	Police: predictive policing ABN AMRO: money laundering prediction
	7.2.2 Adaptive algorithmic brokers	LUMC: predictive tumour modelling MultiCo: predictive people analytics
	7.2.3 The risks of algorithmic brokering	Police: predictive policing
Chapter 8 Changing work	8.2.1 Augmenting work	CB: helpdesk chatbot LUMC: predictive tumour modelling
	8.2.2 Changing responsibilities and control	MultiCo: predictive people analytics Police: predictive policing
	8.2.3 Collective change	CB: helpdesk chatbot KLM: consumption prediction

implies the need for work-related insights, interdisciplinary knowledge, sociotechnical change processes, and ethical awareness in managing AI systems.

1.5   READING GUIDE

Though one of the leading goals of this book is to offer managers tools for managing AI systems in practice, this does not mean that only managers will benefit from reading it. For developers of AI systems, this book provides insight into the importance of collaboration with other parties involved. The challenges we identify at the end of each practical chapter can help you to anticipate the potential obstacles that may lie ahead. Especially in the transition from a technically well-functioning AI system to an AI system embedded in work processes, there are many opportunities for developers, provided that the right approach is taken towards collaboration with managers and users. Chapters 5 and 6 are especially helpful to develop the right stakeholder strategy. In addition, Chapter 7 offers useful tools for thinking about how the outcomes of the developed system can be translated into practice more fundamentally.

For (intended) users of AI systems, this book helps you to prepare for what the system will mean for your work. AI systems are often viewed with suspicion or even fear. With this book we give you a different perspective, in particular in Chapter 8. The practical examples of Chapters 5 and 6 provide insights into what you can do and what knowledge you need, as a user, to allow AI systems to optimally contribute to your work processes, so that work does not become unnecessarily over-automated, but is instead augmented or supported. Involvement in the development of AI systems and openness to what is new are crucial. If you are interested in the technical side of AI, Chapter 7 offers you inspiration by suggesting a new role, the algorithmic broker, where you can combine your domain expertise with more technical knowledge.

For algorithmic brokers bridging domain expertise and technical knowledge, Chapter 7 is especially important. In this chapter, we give examples of the different forms that the role of algorithmic broker can take, and what the advantages and disadvantages can be. Nevertheless, we encourage you to read the rest of the book carefully. To function effectively as an algorithmic broker, an integrated understanding of managing AI systems in practice is important.

For managers, this book is a guide to best practices related to implementing AI systems in your organization. Although it is recommended that you read this book before you start developing and introducing AI in your organization, it is not too late to implement the principles of WISE management even if you have already started. Whether you are a human resources (HR) manager, a sales manager, a production manager, or any other type of manager, this book will help you to understand how to bring AI systems and existing workflows together and the critical role you play in gathering all required expertise. In this book, we will ask a lot from you both in thinking and in action. Our aim is not to deter you, but we do hope to make it clear that the implementation of intelligent systems should not be handled lightly. The key takeaways at the end of each chapter and the recommendations from Chapter 9 will help you to make this challenge concrete and to develop a long-term vision for the WISE management of AI systems in your organization.

Do none of these apply, and are you still interested in our book? Then we hope that you will enjoy reading the coming chapters and that they will bring you new insights.

REFERENCES

Baptista, J., Stein, M.K., Klein, S., Watson-Manheim, M.B., & Lee, J. (2020). Digital work and organisational transformation: Emergent digital/human work configurations in modern organisations. *Journal of Strategic Information Systems*, *29*(2). DOI: 10.1016/j.jsis.2020.101618.

Kim, B., Koopmanschap, I., Mehrizi, M.H.R., Huysman, M., & Ranschaert, E. (2021). How does the radiology community discuss the benefits and limitations of artificial intelligence for their work? A systematic discourse analysis. *European Journal of Radiology*, *136*, 109566.

Nilsson, N. (1971). *Problem-solving methods in artificial intelligence*. New York: McGraw-Hill.

Pachidi, S., Berends, H., Faraj, S., & Huysman, M. (2021). Make way for the algorithms: Symbolic actions and change in a regime of knowing. *Organization Science*, *32*(1), 18–41.

Pesapane, F., Codari, M., & Sardanelli, F. (2018). Artificial intelligence in medical imaging: Threat or opportunity? Radiologists again at the forefront of innovation in medicine. *European Radiology Experimental*, *2*(1), 35–44.

Zhang, Z., Nandhakumar, J., Hummel, J., & Waardenburg, L. (2020). Addressing the key challenges of developing machine learning AI systems for knowledge-intensive work. *MIS Quarterly Executive*, *19*(4), 221–238.

2.   What is AI?

2.1   INTRODUCTION

Ever since 1950, when Alan Turing was the first to wonder whether machines could think (Turing, 1950), AI scientists have been occupied with this question. Yet, artificial intelligence (AI) has only been gaining popularity in recent years and has had more and more consequences for both work and everyday life ever since. One of the main reasons why implementing AI is increasingly interesting for organizations is the large-scale digitization that has taken place in recent years.

Because AI has been in development for such a long time, its history knows many milestones. The various achievements have slowly altered the definition of AI and different techniques have also come into play. Currently, researchers agree that the ability to learn is the central feature that distinguishes AI from other 'intelligent technologies' (such as knowledge management systems). In this chapter we will discuss in detail what this means exactly. We start with an introduction to the history of AI (see Figure 2.1 for a schematic overview of the developments mentioned here), then we discuss different techniques that can be used for AI systems, after which we address the current view of AI and the future of work.

2.2   ORIGINS OF AI

2.2.1   The Start of AI

A historical overview requires a starting point. When it comes to the origins of AI, this is complicated for several reasons. First, AI is seen as part of computer science, which itself emerged from the development of computers. So you can ask yourself: Do we take the origin of computers or merely the AI component as a starting point? From this, the second question immediately follows: If we only take the AI component, what do we count as AI? Finally, it is also true that the history of a concept is not the same as the history of a technology resulting from it. After all, the history of logic and computer science dates back to long before the 1950s. You could say, for example, that George Boole (of Boolean logic, the basis of the digital computer) was already working on

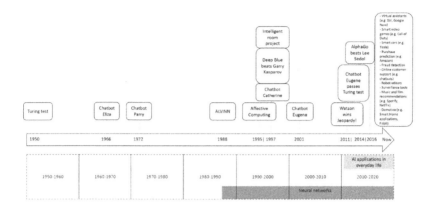

Figure 2.1   Schematic timeline of AI developments

AI, because he codified the logic that eventually became crucial to AI and computer science. If we follow this reasoning, there are many scientists who proved early on to be indispensable for the creation and further development of AI. However, at the time of researchers such as George Boole, there were no cases of a machine that was able to learn and potentially think and act like a human being – the characteristic that has eventually become decisive when determining whether a technology is or is not AI.

Today, AI refers to a technique or system that can perform tasks which can normally only be accomplished by human thinking (Nilsson, 1971; Pesapane et al., 2018). These tasks include facial recognition, voice recognition and decision-making based on context and language skills (such as translation and word recognition). While this was definitely not yet the case in the 1950s and 1960s, this is still considered as the birth period of AI, with mathematician, philosopher and inventor Alan Turing identified as its father. Turing is known to most people as the man who managed to decipher the encrypted messages of the German forces in World War II. Yet, his work mainly revolved around the theme of decision-making in machines.

Turing stated that a human makes a decision based on certain 'extractable' or explicit factors, and he believed that a machine should be able to do that too. Turing developed the so-called 'Turing test', through which one can determine whether a machine is intelligent or not. In the test there are three players: A, B and C. One player, for example player A, is the interrogator. The interrogator directs questions at players B and C, one of whom is a machine. The players cannot see each other and they communicate through text messages. If Player

A cannot distinguish the machine from the human in these messages, the machine is classified as intelligent (Turing, 1950).

There is, however, an issue with the Turing test, since it appeared that people tend to view something as intelligent rather quickly. Consider, for example, one of the first talking bots, Eliza, developed in 1966 by Joseph Weizenbaum at the MIT AI Laboratory (see Figure 2.2). Eliza simulated a psychologist in language and dialogue; she responded to the messages that were typed into the chat with a question or phrase. Eliza was a great success, but was she really intelligent? All her questions and answers were pre-programmed and if you kept chatting with her long enough, her comments would repeat itself.

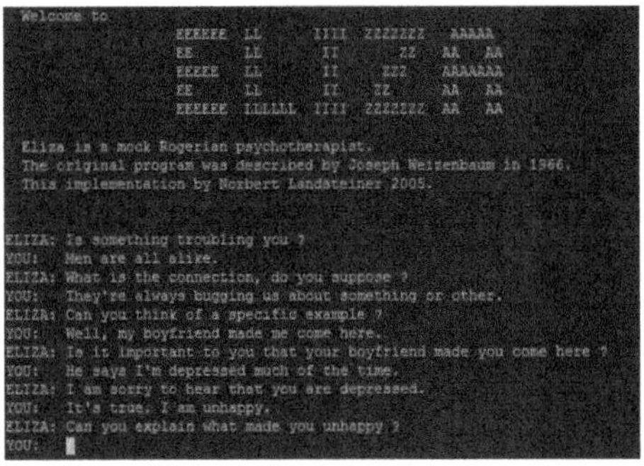

Source: https://commons.wikimedia.org/wiki/File:ELIZA_conversation.png.

Figure 2.2   *Chatbot Eliza*

Although communication was relatively superficial, Eliza was seen as an intelligent system and was an important building block in the development of AI. A number of pre-programmed bots followed after Eliza. In 1972, Parry appeared as Eliza's successor and co-star. Parry played the role of a patient with schizophrenia and followed a script written by psychiatrist Kenneth Colby (Shum et al., 2018). Parry still exists today (see Figure 2.3). At https://www.botlibre.com/browse?id=857177 you can chat with the current version of Parry whenever you want.

Chatbot Catherine emerged in 1997. She was a highly pleasant conversationalist, as long as there was no deviation from the subject of Bill Clinton (Christian, 2011). The chatbot that (according to some) was one of the first to 'really' pass the Turing test was Eugene Goostman. Eugene represented a Ukrainian boy in terms of language. The bot was built in 2001 by Vladimir Veselov and Eugene Demchenko, but it was not until 13 years later that the bot managed to convince a significant part of the jury that he was a real 13-year-old boy (Shah et al., 2016). His stiff way of 'talking' and his grammat-

Figure 2.3   Chatbot Parry in 2021

ical errors were attributed to the culture and language barrier. This historical success is not undisputed, however, as many scientists believe that Eugene should not have passed the test, because his language use was far from being at a human level (Sample and Hern, 2014). Most importantly, what these bots had in common was that they were pre-programmed and therefore could not deal with new topics.

2.2.2   Neural Networks

A major change in the development of AI occurred in the late 1980s with the development of neural networks. These networks are inspired by the human brain and can therefore learn from prior decisions. Solely based on statistics, a neural network comes to a decision and therefore eliminates the need for pre-programming (we will discuss the technical details of neural networks in section 2.3.1).

In 1988, the first self-driving car with this technique was built at Carnegie Mellon University. The car was called ALVINN (Autonomous Land Vehicle In a Neural Network). ALVINN's neural networks used a picture of the road as input to determine in which direction the vehicle should be headed (Pomerleau, 1989). In the years that followed, neural networks have become increasingly central to the development of AI. Through training of neural networks, AI systems can now learn to recognize not only the road but also, for example, traffic lights, zebra crossings and pedestrians. The unique aspect of neural networks is that, in contrast to the time when everything had to be pre-programmed, it can learn on its own.

In 1995, Rosalind Picard of MIT published the article 'Affective comput-ing' (Picard, 1995). This heralded the start of research into 'emotional AI', which means that a computer learns to recognize, understand and simulate emotions. This was a big step towards 'truly' intelligent machines. Two years later, the Intelligent Room Project − also developed at MIT − followed. In this 'intelligent room', computers tracked people's movements and tried to determine from people's gestures whether they were talking to each other or to themselves (Brooks, 1997).

The use of neural networks also resulted in progress in the field of natural language processing (NLP), in which computers are taught to interpret, understand and develop human language. An example of this is IBM's Watson. This system was the result of one of IBM's Grand Challenges and defeated its human opponents in the American television show *Jeopardy!* in 2011. In this game show, Watson had to find the right question for a given answer, which required advanced NLP skills. To achieve this, Watson was given a gigantic amount of 'reading material', namely 200 million pages, including the full contents of Wikipedia and the *World Book Encyclopedia* (Best, 2013). Watson's software, DeepQA, searched for a number of questions for each answer and assigned a score to each option. The question with the highest score won, and so did Watson.

The advent of neural networks did not mean that projects that applied other techniques were immediately discarded. An example of this is IBM's Deep Blue. As many know, this system defeated world chess champion Garry Kasparov in 1997. While this milestone is often mentioned in the AI list, the software used back then had nothing to do with AI as we know it today. The advanced chip used in Deep Blue was able to calculate successful chess moves at high speed. The strategy involved was the so-called 'brute force' strategy; a technique that has little to do with intelligence, but is mainly based on computing power. This category is therefore also called 'symbolic AI' (Greenemeier, 2017).

The possibilities offered by the use of neural networks become visible when we compare Deep Blue's victory to the victory of the organization DeepMinds. Almost 20 years after Deep Blue's triumph, the organization (which was bought by Google in 2014) ventured into the Chinese board game Go. The game Go has 300 times more gameplay than a game of chess and is therefore much more complex. When a player starts, one has a choice of 361 different moves, compared to 20 moves in chess. After the first move, chess has 400 follow-up options, while Go has about 129 960. After two moves, this number becomes 71 852 in chess and about 17 billion in Go, and so on (Susskind, 2020). The AI system, called AlphaGo, worked with four neural networks in order to first learn on its own how to play the game. Building on 30 million previous Go games, it played against itself to learn to predict a good move. In 2016, AlphaGo defeated human world champion Lee Sedol.

2.2.3   AI Applications in Everyday Life

Since 2011, AI is no longer reserved for academics doing research and for playing games, but is increasingly used in daily life. Due to, for example, improved bandwidth and the introduction of cloud hosting, it is now possible to install voice assistants such as Siri, Google Now and Cortana on smartphones. The neural networks at the heart of such voice assistants make sure that they get better the more these voice assistants are used. Many similar assistants are now for sale – such as Alexa and Google Home – and AI is no longer merely an academic experiment, but also a common product that can adapt to new situations remarkably quickly.

The potential market value and practical applications of AI have also been noticed by organizations and consumers, and it has managed to expand into the public sector. Thanks to various techniques, such as neural networks, the impact of AI is increasing. Performance has improved, but the number of segments of society where AI can be deployed has also increased as a result of this development. Image processing by means of neural networks is no longer only important for self-driving cars, but also for medical purposes, for example. Advanced search engines cannot exist without NLP. In the following sections, we take a closer look at the specific techniques that can be used to develop AI systems.

2.3   AI TECHNIQUES

As described above, AI generally refers to a technique or system that can perform tasks that can normally only be accomplished by human thinking. These tasks include facial recognition, voice recognition, context-based decision-making, and language skills (for example, translation and word recognition). There are various research areas within AI for performing these tasks (see Table 2.1). In contrast to previous technologies such as knowledge management systems, AI systems have the capacity to learn. Because neural networks are most commonly considered to be the driving force behind AI systems, we first describe what this technique means. However, this is not the only method through which systems can learn. After neural networks, we therefore pay attention to what machine learning more generally means, and what forms it can take.

2.3.1   The Techniques behind Neural Networks

Neural networks are made to resemble the networks of the human brain. Roughly estimated, the human brain contains about 100 billion neurons (an interesting comparison is that this number of neurons is approximately the same as the number of stars in our galaxy). Each neuron is connected to about 1000 other neurons. Those points of contact are called synapses and synaptic connections, where the information is stored.

Table 2.1   *Overview of AI fields*

AI-field	Focus area	Example
Knowledge representation and reasoning	How expert knowledge can be translated into code	Expert systems
Planning and search	Planning and scheduling problems involving one or multiple actors	AlphaGo
Computer vision	Image recognition and image classification	Facial recognition software, Facebook's 'friend' tagging
Natural language processing	Interpreting, understanding and developing human language	IBM Watson
Information gathering	Connecting humans and information	Search engines, recommendation systems

Source: Based on AIREA-NL (2019).

In an artificial neural network, just like in the brain, different neurons are connected to each other and can therefore influence each other's behaviour. To use the terminology of the human brain's neural network in the case of an artificial neural network, we can imagine it as a collection of dots connected by lines (see Figure 2.4). The dots are the neurons, the lines are the synaptic connections. Where the dots connect with the lines are the synapses.

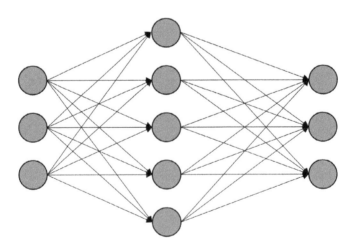

Figure 2.4   *Schematic example of a neural network*

The model that is currently most commonly used for an artificial neural network contains a number for each neuron and for each synapse. Each neuron can adjust its state (at regular intervals) by taking the weighted average of the input from all neurons it is connected to. The strength of the synapses determines the weight of each neuron in this calculation. In addition, a so-called feedforward network is often deployed, whereby information is passed on in only one direction. Such a feedforward network includes different layers of neurons, with an upper layer that receives the information and a bottom layer that executes the processed information (Tegmark, 2017, pp. 106–108).

Figure 2.5 schematically shows a feedforward neural network for facial recognition. All incoming images are entered as pixels in the top layer. In the next layer, it analyses the coarse facial features. In the layer below, the recognized facial features become more refined and it can, for example, already recognize an eye or an ear. In the layer underneath, the facial features become even finer and faces can be distinguished. From there it can also come up with suggestions as to who was initially entered as pixels.

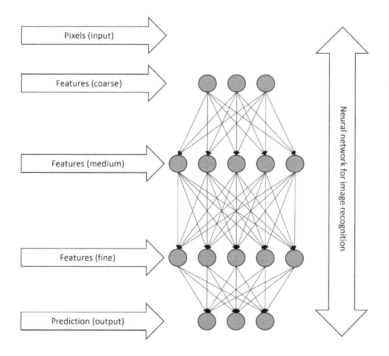

Figure 2.5   Feedforward neural network

In this respect, artificial neural networks are certainly nowhere near the point of approaching human brains. In fact, the question is whether they will ever be, since our knowledge about the functioning of the brain itself is not (yet) complete; the neurons in the human brain are complex electrochemical mechanisms which are still being examined to this day. It is therefore all the more surprising to realize that AI researchers have already shown that relatively simple, simulated neurons – all identical, and whose operation consists of only a few simple rules – can perform complex tasks; sometimes even at the same level as a person (for example, Watson and AlphaGo, see section 2.2.2). The ability of the network to learn from previous examples and from success and failure lies at the heart of this. This can also be achieved through using techniques other than neural networks. All these techniques, including neural networks, are grouped under the header of 'machine learning'.

2.3.2   Machine Learning

Machine learning is an area of research within the AI field focused on developing algorithms – a series of coded instructions aimed at solving an arithmetic problem – that can improve through experience; in other words, have the capacity to learn (Tegmark, 2017, p. 106). It uses statistical methods to generate predictions and make decisions. In machine learning, and specifically deep learning, neural networks are trained with datasets, allowing them to learn from this data and subsequently make decisions. Such 'intelligent' systems can be used for various purposes. Depending on the objective and the associated tasks, algorithms are trained in different ways, whereby generalization and optimization are of central importance (Brunskill, 2019). Generalization refers to solving new problems with more general information. This is important because we cannot feed all possible cases or examples of a problem or issue to the algorithm so that it could learn from this. Optimization refers to the intention that an AI system performs the task as well as possible and therefore makes the best decision with the information available. Algorithms can be trained in four different ways: by means of supervised learning, unsupervised learning, generative adversarial networks or reinforcement learning. We discuss these options below.

Supervised learning
With supervised learning, the dataset to be used is labelled, which means that it has already been indicated what each data point entails. As a result, the dataset used for supervised learning contains both the properties and the outcome of what needs to be predicted or recognized. Because the algorithm used has examples of data in which characteristics are labeled, it can recognize new data points and classify it automatically. Essentially, the following happens: if X is

a data point and Y is its label, then the algorithm is supposed to categorize all X as Y (Yeung et al., 2017). More specifically, suppose the data point X is a fork, then this data point has been labelled (Y) 'fork'. The algorithm must then be able to recognize that all kinds of forks belong to the label 'fork'. Training the algorithm with a dataset in which as many forks as possible are labelled optimizes the algorithm which will then (if all goes well) distinguish all forks from other objects.

Because the dataset in supervised learning always contains the intended result, with this technique you can always compare the resulting predictions with reality after training a model, making it possible to calculate the accuracy of the model. For this purpose, the original dataset is usually split into 80 per cent training data (to train the model) and 20 per cent test data (to validate the prediction quality of the model).

It must be made clear that supervised learning is a form of machine learning that does not necessarily make use of a neural network. It is generally used for regression, where a value or number is predicted; or classification, where a group or category is predicted. This means that a linear regression or a logistic regression (in which a series of numbers is converted into a value between 0 and 1) can also be used for supervised learning. In contrast, rule-based classification does not fall under supervised learning. Hereby an algorithm can classify data on the basis of rules, and no 'learning' is involved.

The first AI systems that emerged in the 1950s were supervised learning algorithms. In that period, the resulting models were mainly used for pattern recognition in data. To this day, the majority of all AI systems that are being developed still work with supervised learning. A recognizable example is the algorithm used by Facebook for recognizing 'friends' in our photos. In this case, we provided the labels in the dataset ourselves, by tagging our friends for years. Now, this is no longer necessary, because the algorithm has learned how to classify.

Unsupervised learning
In unsupervised learning, the dataset has no labels. Instead, the algorithm itself tries to cluster the data on the basis of underlying patterns. There are roughly three types of algorithms for unsupervised learning: clustering algorithms, dimensionality reduction and association algorithms.

In clustering, data is sorted on the basis of common characteristics. To return to the example of the forks: in unsupervised learning, the algorithm itself determines that there are certain objects with three teeth (forks) and objects with a smooth blade (knives). The objects with three teeth have more in common with other objects with three teeth than those with a smooth blade. In this way, the objects with three teeth form a cluster and the objects with a smooth blade form another cluster. These clusters can then be used in a subsequent analysis (Data Science Partners, 2020).

In the case of dimensionality reduction, this is specifically about reducing the number of properties present in a dataset. The algorithm combines several properties under one denominator. An example of this could be that the algorithm summarizes all dogs with a brown-black coat, triangular ears, a long nose and a long tail under the label 'shepherd' (Data Science Partners, 2020). This means that four traits in a dataset are reduced to one.

Association algorithms, also referred to as association rule learning, sort data on the basis of their relationship with other data points (Alpaydin, 2020). This mainly focuses on underlying relationships in transaction data. An example of this is an algorithm that predicts which products a customer will also like when they order something from an online shop.

In unsupervised learning, an algorithm thus tries to recognize a hidden underlying structure and sort data on the basis of that structure. This technique is not yet as widely used as supervised learning, especially because unsupervised learning requires an even larger amount of data to be able to learn. In addition, with unsupervised learning there is no possibility to validate predictions and measure reliability, which makes it more difficult to apply this technique in practice. Currently, we mainly see examples of unsupervised learning in online shops and social media.

Generative adversarial networks
Generative adversarial networks (GAN) is a method that is a subgroup of unsupervised learning. These networks are able to create their own dataset based on the training dataset, and can then recognize other patterns in this new dataset. With this technique, two models are trained simultaneously: a generative network and a discriminative network. The purpose of a generative network is to produce data that is as realistic as possible, so that the discriminative network cannot distinguish it from 'real' data. The aim of the discriminative network is precisely to distinguish the real data from 'false' data (Goodfellow, 2016).

In the paper 'Generative adversarial sets' (Goodfellow et al., 2014), Ian Goodfellow and his colleagues use the following analogy to illustrate this concept: the generative model can be compared to a gang of forgers trying to use x number of fake coins. The discriminatory model can be compared to the police who need to distinguish a fake coin from a real one. Since both models are opponents of each other, they are called adversarial networks. In addition, the models will also improve each other, due to the competitive element in their relationship. In other words, the generative network will increasingly produce real data, and the discriminative network will become more skilled at distinguishing fake and real data (Goodfellow et al., 2014).

GAN is only used sporadically. The most famous examples are Instagram influencers such as Lil' Miquela, who don't actually exist.[1] As it can generate photos of, for example, faces, bedrooms or cars that never existed, GAN has also been compared to idea machines. However, a limit to GAN systems is that they can never 'think' completely out of the box. In other words: 'When a [GAN] system is trained to create photos of cars, it will never make a refrigerator' (Duursma, 2020).

Reinforcement learning

Reinforcement learning works by means of reward and punishment. The most important aspects of reinforcement learning are optimization and generalization, and delayed consequences and exploration (Brunskill, 2019). We have already described optimization and generalization at the beginning of this section. Delayed consequences and exploration are aspects that do not occur in the other forms of machine learning, and precisely these aspects ensure that algorithms might ultimately become faster, better and smarter than a human being.

The delayed consequences aspect entails that the consequences of individual actions of the algorithm are not immediately labelled as right or wrong. In general, machine learning is often used to solve a planning problem. This is a future problem, where the individual actions together can ultimately lead to a successful or unsuccessful outcome. While other machine learning methods involve assessing individual actions, reinforcement learning postpones the reward or punishment for a particular choice until the end of the process (Hogervorst, 1991). The assessment of an action only becomes clear after a series of choices, so that the algorithm learns to recognize not only the correct action, but also the correct series of choices.

With regard to exploration, reinforcement learning resembles how a child would achieve a new skill. The algorithm receives a dataset and tries to find out for itself what a good outcome is. An example of this is learning the Atari game of Pong. A dataset of all possible choices and moves that can be made is provided to an algorithm. The algorithm then plays against a human and, in this way, learns which moves or choices yield points and which do not. Initially, the algorithm does many things wrong, because it makes random choices. Besides that, it will occasionally make good choices by accident. The algorithm remembers those good choices and thereby eventually learns the right and most optimal way to perform a task (Tegmark, 2017).

The advantage of reinforcement learning over other machine learning methods is that an algorithm can ultimately learn to perform better than a human, because it does not – as is especially the case with supervised learning – only learn the things that a human being has already demonstrated or prepared. Although this technique could hold great promise for the future of AI, it is currently only used in a very limited way (mainly due to the high margin of error at the start of development).

2.3.3   Artificial General Intelligence

All the forms of machine learning methods discussed above have one thing in common: they are narrow, which means they are trained for a specific task. However, here too, many AI scientists have greater ambitions and hope to be able to get to a point where an algorithm can be used for more than one task and can – just like a human being – switch between tasks. This is commonly referred to as artificial general intelligence (AGI) and is often seen as the 'dot on the horizon' of AI scientists. It is a form of AI that 'equals and surpasses human intelligence' and that 'can achieve almost any objective, including learning new things, [which is] in contrast to, for example, the limited intelligence of a chess program' (Tegmark, 2017, p. 48).

AGI does not yet exist. In fact, AI scientists themselves disagree about when or if it will happen. While optimists such as Larry Page and Richard Sutton think this is a feasible and even desirable goal within a period of 20 to 100 years, sceptics such as former MIT professor Rodney Brooks (who also invented the Roomba vacuum cleaner) argue that AGI is so difficult to realize that it will not happen in hundreds of years (Tegmark, 2017, pp. 50–52). One of the conditions for developing AGI is that scientists must find a way to equip machines with consciousness. And this is precisely one of the biggest problems, because (just like the functioning of the human brain) science as we know it cannot explain human consciousness.

The AI system that comes closest to any form of AGI so far is 'K', a supercomputer built by Fujitsu (Reece, 2020). Although the computer was named the fastest in the world in 2011, with this supercomputer – consisting of 82 944 processors – it took 40 minutes to simulate a single second of neural activity (Hornyak, 2013). The chance that AGI will become a reality in the near future therefore seems very small.

2.4   SUMMARY

In this chapter, we discussed what it means exactly when we speak of AI. AI is becoming an increasingly popular concept. There is even talk of an 'AI-hype'. Yet, there is still a lot of debate as to whether a technology is 'AI or not'. Given the historical developments, this is not surprising. Over time, various definitions and techniques have been raised and debated, which have not contributed to a clarification of boundaries.

In section 2.2 we described that AI has been in development for almost 70 years. In these years it has become increasingly advanced, and therefore the concept was also subject to alteration. What is more, as we described in section 2.3, various (statistical) techniques can be applied. These different techniques, however, have one aspect in common: AI systems can learn.

With the increasing availability of data, this learning capacity is expanded further and, as we have seen in section 2.3, becomes increasingly complex. A consequence of this increasing complexity is that we can understand less and less about how the technology works; in other words, AI systems are increasingly black-boxed. This has major consequences for work and organization, which we will return to several times in this book.

For the time being, the AI systems that we encounter in our daily lives will still remain narrow, limited to performing one task or focused on a single goal. Nonetheless, the risks of AI are increasingly being pointed out, with job losses at the top of the list. In the next chapter, we explore these current perspectives on AI and the future of work.

NOTE

1. https://www.instagram.com/p/CDHvUkWHqw-/?igshid=kfx4iran4n3j.

REFERENCES

AIREA-NL (2019). *Artificial intelligence research agenda for the Netherlands.* NWO.

Alpaydin, E. (2020). *Introduction to machine learning* (4th edn). Cambridge, MA: MIT Press.

Best, J. (2013) IBM Watson: The inside story of how the Jeopardy-winning supercomputer was born, and what it wants to do next. https://www.techrepublic.com/article/ibm-watson-the-inside-story-of-how-the-jeopardy-winning-supercomputer-was-born-and-what-it-wants-to-do-next/.

Brooks, R.A. (1997). The intelligent room project. In: *Proceedings of the Second International Conference on Cognitive Technology Humanizing the Information Age* (pp. 271–278). IEEE.

Brunskill, E. (2019). Reinforcement learning, winter 2019, Lecture 1. https://www.youtube.com/watch?v=FgzM3zpZ55o.

Christian, B. (2011). Mind vs. machine. https://www.theatlantic.com/magazine/archive/2011/03/mind-vs-machine/308386/?utm_source=share&utm_campaign=share.

Data Science Partners (2020). Unsupervised learning: Wat is het? https://pythoncursus.nl/unsupervised-learning/.

Duursma, J. (2020). Generative adversarial network. https://www.jarnoduursma.nl/wat-is-een-generative-adversarial-network/.

Goodfellow, I.J. (2016). Introduction to GANs, NIPS 2016. https://www.youtube.com/watch?v=9JpdAg6uMXs.

Goodfellow, I.J., Pouget-Abadie, J., Mirza, M., Xu, B., Warde-Farley, D., et al. (2014). Generative adversarial nets. In *Proceedings of the 27th International Conference on Neural Information Processing Systems – Volume 2* (pp. 2672–2680).

Greenemeier, L. (2017). 20 Years after Deep Blue: How AI has advanced since con-
quering chess. https://www.scientificamerican.com/article/20-years-after-deep-blue
-how-ai-has-advanced-since-conquering-chess/.

Hogervorst, A. (1991). Reinforcement learning. *Kennisgeving*, *4*(2), 12–15.

Hornyak, T. (2013). Fujitsu supercomputer simulates 1 second of brain activity. https://
www.cnet.com/news/fujitsu-supercomputer-simulates-1-second-of-brain-activity/.

Nilsson, N. (1971). *Problem-solving methods in artificial intelligence.* New York:
McGraw-Hill.

Pesapane, F., Codari, M., & Sardanelli, F. (2018). Artificial intelligence in medical
imaging: Threat or opportunity? Radiologists again at the forefront of innovation in
medicine. *European Radiology Experimental*, *2*(1), 35–44.

Picard, R.W. (1995). *Affective computing.* MIT Media Laboratory Perceptual
Computing Section Technical Report No. 321, Cambridge, MA, 2139.

Pomerleau, D. (1989). ALVINN: An Autonomous Land Vehicle in a Neural Network.
Advances in Neural Information Processing Systems, 305–313.

Reece, S. (2020). What are the 3 types of AI? A guide to narrow, general, and super
artificial intelligence. https://codebots.com/artificial-intelligence/the-3-types-of-ai
-is-the-third-even-possible.

Sample, I., & Hern, A. (2014). Scientists dispute whether computer 'Eugene Goostman'
passed Turing test. https://www.theguardian.com/technology/2014/jun/09/scientists
-disagree-over-whether-turing-test-has-been-passed.

Shah, H., Warwick, K., Vallverdú, J., & Wu, D. (2016). Can machines talk?
Comparison of Eliza with modern dialogue systems. *Computers in Human Behavior*,
58, 278–295.

Shum, H.Y., He, X.D., & Li, D. (2018). From Eliza to XiaoIce: Challenges and opportunities with social chatbots. *Frontiers of Information Technology and Electronic
Engineering*, *19*(1), 10–26.

Susskind, D. (2020). *A world without work.* London: Allen Lane.

Tegmark, M. (2017). *Life 3.0 Mens zijn in het tijdperk van kunstmatige intelligentie.*
Amsterdam: Maven Publishing.

Turing, A.M. (1950). Computing machinery and intelligence. *Mind*, *49*, 433–460.

Yeung, S., Ramanathan, V., Russakovsky, O., Shen, L., Mori, G., & Fei-Fei, L. (2017).
Learning to learn from noisy web videos. In *Proceedings of the IEEE Conference on
Computer Vision and Pattern Recognition* (pp. 5154–5162).

3.   Perspectives on AI and work

3.1   INTRODUCTION

In Chapter 2, we addressed the various techniques that can be used for developing artificial intelligence (AI) systems. Due to the unique ability of AI to perform knowledge-related tasks, which can normally only be done by humans, it should come as no surprise that the possible consequences of these systems for work and organizations are increasingly discussed. Because AI systems are more and more able to generate decisions and suggestions based on large datasets, these capabilities are expected to create a variety of opportunities for organizations, not only in terms of efficiency, productivity and cost reduction (Newell and Marabelli, 2015), but also in terms of objectivity and consistent decision-making (Barrett and Oborn, 2013; Zarsky, 2016).

On the other hand, warnings about the possible negative consequences of AI to work have also increased in recent years. This mainly concerns the chance that AI systems can take over a large number of jobs. This is no longer merely about administrative functions (as was the case with prior information technologies, such as expert systems), but also about knowledge-intensive, professional tasks. The predicted numbers regarding job loss vary. Frey and Osborne published an article in 2013 in which they predicted that 47 per cent of current jobs could be taken over (Frey and Osborne, 2013, 2017); later estimates are more nuanced. Rather than jobs, these focus on tasks, with predictions heading towards 9 per cent job loss (e.g., Felten et al., 2018; Forrester Research, 2017; OECD, 2016).

The increased focus on tasks as a unit of analysis means that more and more attention is currently being paid to specific areas of work where AI will have an impact. Subsequently, the possible consequences for work and organizations as mentioned in recent research can be summarized under three themes: (1) changes to knowledge work and expertise; (2) new forms of control; and (3) changes to knowledge gathering and learning.

3.2   CHANGES TO KNOWLEDGE WORK AND EXPERTISE

Which aspects of human work can be taken over by AI systems – and whether this is possible at all – is a discussion that has been around almost as long as the first AI developments in the 1950s (e.g., Dreyfus, 1967). Given the developments in AI techniques as described in Chapter 2, we cannot deny that routine, cognitive tasks that are well defined and can therefore be reduced to a set of rules are likely to be taken over by AI systems (Susskind, 2020). In addition, tasks that are more dependent on what we call expertise or tacit knowledge, where part of the knowledge often cannot be explained directly (Polanyi, 1966), are also increasingly subjected to the use of AI (Faraj et al., 2018). Think of recognizing an image, for example. In general, this is not an activity that people can describe according to clear rules. Yet, algorithms already exist that, for specific tasks, can do this better than humans (Esteva et al., 2017). For this type of work, where expertise is an important aspect, it is now even said that about 30 per cent of the tasks can be taken over by AI systems (Manyika et al., 2017). The challenge for organizations is to understand which tasks this entails and what this means for the existing work (Faraj et al., 2018; Huysman, 2020).

For organizations, the challenge lies in retaining sufficient expertise, when parts of that expertise can be taken over by AI systems within the foreseeable future. Since AI systems are still far from being able to take over everything, some of the work will still have to be done by human experts. But how do you keep experts motivated to preserve their skill level if they can no longer execute some of the tasks that belong to their area of expertise?

This development also poses a challenge for experts themselves. A mainstream and well-accepted idea is that experts (for example, pianists, surgeons) need at least 10 000 hours of practice to build up sufficient expertise (Gladwell, 2008). Achieving those training hours becomes difficult when, half the time, the work is done by an AI system. Consider, for example, surgical robots taking over simple operations from surgical staff. This may sound attractive at first, as it can be cost-effective or time-saving, but what does it actually mean for the fine motor skills of the surgeon? Recent studies point to mixed consequences for the expertise of medical students when they are taught partly by means of a robot (Beane, 2018), and to changes in coordination when surgery teams use such a robot (Sergeeva et al., 2020).

A counter-argument to the loss of expertise is that, because AI systems can take over more routine tasks, employees are given more time and space to deal with the more complex issues for which they actually need their expertise and can optimally utilize it. Although this may appear to be a valid argument at first, for these employees it also means a higher level of specialization and more complex work (Faraj et al., 2018). Such requirements can have long-term consequences for the minimum education level of the employees, with a corresponding increase in salary. It is therefore important for organizations not only to be concerned with the short-term efficiency and productivity of an AI system, but also to consider the long-term effects for the expertise of their employees.

Finally, a common question regarding the use of AI systems to perform parts of the work is: Who is then responsible for its consequences? Do factory managers receive a bonus if the factory, based on algorithmic forecasts, produces in excess of its target at the end of the year? And do doctors receive honourable mentions if, by means of an AI system, they are able to detect a tumour that is hidden from view? Conversely, should factory managers be summoned by their bosses if predictions were not entirely correct and the factory has performed below its target? Are doctors held responsible if the AI system misdiagnoses a patient?

It is often emphasized that AI systems can also make mistakes, and that experts must therefore make the final judgement (Lupton and Juttel, 2015). However, to make such a choice might require different responsibilities of the experts, and probably has consequences for the use of AI systems. Organizations are therefore required to perform a balancing act in which they have to weigh and compare often incomparable consequences.

3.3   NEW FORMS OF CONTROL

The use of AI systems gives organizations an increasing need and legitimacy for the collection and use of internal and external data. More and more work processes and activities of employees and the organization are expressed in numbers. This can lead to improved insights into who and what is of value. On the other hand, the negative result is that it seems to limit the freedom of employees and sometimes also organizations (e.g., Ananny, 2016; Orlikowski and Scott, 2016).

AI systems can provide a concrete prediction or expectation about the output to be delivered by employees via complex statistical calculations (see Chapter 2). Initial studies in this area point to the consequences of disrupting the balance between professional freedom and organizational control (e.g., Kellogg et al., 2020). For instance, only recently it became known that Amazon employees are assessed by how much time exists between finding a package in the warehouse and the shipment of this package, which largely limits their freedom of movement. These insights have led to redundancies, with many disgruntled employees and plenty of negative press as a result.[1] In addition, organizations such as TripAdvisor, with their ratings of hotels and restaurants, have a fundamental influence on the success of companies in the tourism sector.

Collecting and using data and managing by means of numbers and predictions thus has two sides. On the one hand, it maps the work processes that are central to an organization, through which the value of the employee can be made visible. On the other hand, the visibility of these work processes can turn against the employee, recording and reviewing every action down to the last minute.

It is increasingly stated that organizations need to be aware of the importance of a balance between professional freedom and organizational control. This balance is important because, for example, employees can come up with so-called workarounds, where the data that is collected does not reflect reality. Studies have already shown how journalists tactically upload 'quick-and-dirty articles' to increase their publication score (Christin, 2020), and how employees are often influenced by what numbers they think management expects from them when completing work activities (Cunha and Carugati, 2018).

Studies also indicate that the assumptions made in data collection by, for example, management determine what ultimately becomes visible in data (a so-called self-fulfilling prophecy). For example, if an organization decides to conduct data collection in line with existing work protocols, it will not be visible whether this protocol works or not, or how often it is deviated from. Initial studies in this area have examined medical personnel and indicated that they often perform treatment steps in a different order than the protocol order based upon which they must report in their data system (Pine and Liboiron, 2015). It is even pointed out that having to follow such rigid systems when reporting on their work can affect the creativity and flexibility of teams (Pine and Mazmanian, 2017). Organizations face a challenge in determining when collecting and using data actually hinders the work processes, or may even be a form of false control.

3.4   CHANGES TO KNOWLEDGE ACQUISITION AND LEARNING

Several studies that looked at knowledge gathering in organizations now indicate that the use of AI systems makes it easier to visualize work patterns. As a result, choices and ideas that impact upon the performance of an organization can be better visualized, which can benefit the objectivity of the organizational processes. These studies emphasize that when AI systems are deployed to find and adjust work patterns, this improves knowledge gathering and the opportunity for organizations to learn and improve (e.g., Nikolaidis and Shah, 2012; Sachon and Boquet, 2017; Shah et al., 2011).

Not everyone agrees with this perspective. Through the application of AI systems, organizations may run the risk of missing precisely those outliers that are necessary for innovation (Pachidi and Huysman, 2016). In Chapter 2, we have already discussed the current narrow characteristic of AI systems, causing them to merely perform the task they were trained for. Through the use of the current narrow AI systems, unexpected success, different perspectives and groundbreaking insights from revolutionaries such as Steve Jobs are out of the question (Pachidi and Huysman, 2016). In such cases, it is argued that:

> In order to innovate and to survive in highly volatile environments, organizations also need to apply 'technologies of foolishness' (March, 1988), being open to new alternatives by employing playfulness, trial and error, and improvisation. Acting irrationally can sometimes lead to great outcomes for the organization. The organization needs to have some Don Quixote's [*sic*], the people who may seem crazy by deviating from the expected behaviour and remaining open to unexpected consequences (March and Weill, 2009) ... Not only should organizations reduce their high expectations regarding what [AI systems] bring to organizational intelligence, it would be smart to include technologies of foolishness when engaging in learning. (Pachidi and Huysman, 2016, p. 9)

Another AI-specific property that calls the possibilities for knowledge acquisition and learning for organizations into question is the so-called black-boxed nature of these systems (Burrell, 2016; Faraj et al., 2018). However useful algorithms can be, people are often not aware of their exact functioning and do not know how a certain outcome is achieved. The problem is that in AI systems, decision-making increasingly rests with the learning algorithm and not with the programmer (Mittelstadt et al., 2016). This means that even if someone tells you exactly what the dataset entails and which inputs have been used, it is difficult to find out why the algorithm arrived at a given result. Instead of organization-wide insights, perhaps only a few individuals – for example, highly specialized programmers – can actually grasp the results of an AI system (Faraj et al., 2018). The question therefore is: To what extent can organizations really use the results of AI systems in order to learn?

Also, not everyone agrees about the objectivity of those results. More and more researchers are emphasizing that algorithms are not objective entities, but are written (that is, coded) by programmers with certain views, opinions and habits. Whether consciously or unconsciously, such subjective properties are also coded into the algorithm by the programmers (Introna, 2016) and can affect how a dataset – which is used to train the algorithm – is constructed. As a result, an algorithm can, for example, take on a political orientation that has an impact on the decision-making process. An example of this is the order or arrangement of web pages. How important a page is depends on whether and how the page's keywords are regarded by the algorithm. How such an algorithm is programmed, and what value it attaches to a certain set of words compared to another set, determines which page will be at the top (Introna and Nissenbaum, 2000).

While, on the one hand, more and more hope is placed on increasing the objectivity and efficiency of knowledge gathering, on the other hand this is strongly called into question. The consequences of the use of AI systems for knowledge gathering and learning for organizations is therefore far from clear, and the question remains: What knowledge can AI systems offer organizations?

3.5   RESPONSIBLE AI

In recent years, the almost limitless possibilities, but also the concerns about the unforeseen consequences of AI for work, organizations and society as a whole, have led to more and more talk about so-called 'responsible AI'. Ethical questions regarding the development and influence of AI systems are key in this topic.[2] Until recently, most of the attention in this debate was focused on legal solutions. These solutions unanimously emphasize the need to limit the use of inscrutable, black-boxed algorithms by governments and organizations in order to minimize their negative effects.

Recently, increasing attention has also been paid to the more technical aspects of responsible AI, in which explainability has become key. It is expected that better explainability will lead to more transparent and more reliable AI systems (Doran et al., 2017; Gunning, 2017; Santiago and Escrig, 2017). A consequence of the shift in attention towards explainability is that more and more computer scientists and AI developers are working on developing technical applications that make the complex algorithms 'explainable' and 'interpretable' (Hafermalz and Huysman, 2019).

At the moment, researchers doubt whether adding a technical aspect to the focus on legal solutions is sufficiently comprehensive. They suggest that not only the system itself (and therefore the technical aspect), but especially the social context, should be organized in such a way that AI can be used in a responsible manner (Dignum, 2019). The central point is that: 'Responsible Artificial Intelligence is about human responsibility for the development of intelligent systems along fundamental human principles and values, to ensure human flourishing and well-being in a sustainable world' (Dignum, 2019, p. 119).

Responsible AI thus means that responsibility goes further than the technical and legal details regarding AI development. Instead, its implementation and use are also a key part of this. Hence, responsible AI is about developing, implementing and using AI in ways that do justice to humanity, while respecting social values and moral and ethical considerations.

Although the pursuit of such responsible AI seems like a worthy objective, little is known about what this means in practice. Moving forward with responsible development, implementation and use of AI requires 'methods that clarify responsibilities and clarify the choices for the development, data and origin of knowledge, the [work] process and the stakeholders' (Dignum, 2019, p. 119). With this book, we aim to take a first step in that direction by providing insight into the choices and challenges associated with managing AI in practice.

3.6   SUMMARY

More attention is being paid to the influence of AI systems on work and organizations. With tasks as the unit of analysis, in this chapter we have described where the greatest changes with regard to work and organizations are expected. At the same time, our description illustrates that there are also many uncertainties. We described the recent shift in focus to responsible AI as an answer to, or in preparation for, the uncertainty surrounding the consequences of AI for work, organizations and society as a whole. The first steps have been taken, but there is still a long way to go.

A central point in all studies discussed in this chapter is that little is known about the development, implementation and use of AI in practice and in the context of organizations. What is really happening in organizations that have chosen to develop and implement an AI system? With this book we address this by tapping into the insights we have obtained from eight cases. We will describe these in detail in the next five chapters. In Chapter 4 we first provide a general introduction to each case. Next, in Chapters 5 to 8 we discuss the four most common themes and associated challenges that we encountered. In this way, we provide tools for managing AI in practice.

NOTES

1.   For example: https://futurism.com/amazon-ai-fire-workers.
2.   High Level Expert Group on AI Ethics Guidelines for Trustworthy AI (2019).

REFERENCES

Ananny, M. (2016). Toward an ethics of algorithms: Convening, observation, probability, and timeliness. *Science, Technology and Human Values, 41*(1), 93–117.
Barrett, M., & Oborn, E. (2013). Envisioning E-HRM and strategic HR: Taking seriously identity, innovation practice, and service. *Journal of Strategic Information Systems, 22*(3), 252–256.
Beane, M. (2018). Shadow learning: Building robotic surgical skill when approved means fail. *Administrative Science Quarterly, 64*(1), 87–123.

Burrell, J. (2016). How the machine 'thinks': Understanding opacity in machine learning algorithms. *Big Data and Society*, *3*(1), 1–12.

Christin, A. (2020). *Metrics at work: Journalism and the contested meaning of algorithms.* Princeton, NJ: Princeton University Press.

Cunha, J., & Carugati, A. (2018). Transfiguration work and the system of transfiguration: How employees represent and misrepresent their work. *MIS Quarterly*, *42*(3), 873–894.

Dignum, V. (2019). *Responsible artificial intelligence.* Cham: Springer.

Doran, D., Schulz, S., & Besold, T.R. (2017). What does explainable AI really mean? A new conceptualization of perspectives. arXiv preprint arXiv:1710.00794.

Dreyfus, H.L. (1967). Why computers must have bodies in order to be intelligent. *Review of Metaphysics*, *21*(1), 13–32

Esteva, A., Kuprel, B., Novoa, R.A., Ko, J., Swetter, S.M., et al. (2017). Dermatologist-level classification of skin cancer with deep neural networks. *Nature*, *542*(7639), 115–118.

Faraj, S., Pachidi, S., & Sayegh, K. (2018). Working and organizing in the age of the learning algorithm. *Information and Organization*, *28*(1), 62–70.

Felten, E.W., Raj, M., & Seamans, R. (2018). A method to link advances in Artificial Intelligence to occupational abilities. *AEA Papers and Proceedings*, 108, 54–57.

Forrester Research (2017). *The future of jobs, 2027: Working side by side with robots.* New York: Forrester Research.

Frey, C.B., & Osborne, M.A. (2013). The future of employment. How susceptible are jobs to computerisation. http://sep4u.gr/wp-content/uploads/The_Future_of_Employment_ox_2013.pdf.

Frey, C.B., & Osborne, M.A. (2017). The future of employment: how susceptible are jobs to computerisation? *Technological Forecasting and Social Change*, *114*, 254–280.

Gladwell, M. (2008). *Outliers: The story of success.* New York: Little Brown.

Gunning, D. (2017). Explainable artificial intelligence (XAI): Defense Advanced Research Projects Agency. https://www.darpa.mil/program/explainable-artificial-intelligence.

Hafermalz, E., & Huysman, M.H. (2019). Please explain: Looking under the hood of explainable AI. Paper presented at PROS 2019, Understanding the Dynamics of Work, Innovation, and Collective Action, Crete.

Huysman, M. (2020). Information systems research on artificial intelligence and work: A commentary on 'Robo-Apocalypse cancelled? Reframing the automation and future of work debate'. *Journal of Information Technology*, *35*(4), 307–309.

Introna, L.D. (2016). Algorithms, governance, and governmentality: On governing academic writing. *Science, Technology, and Human Values*, *41*(1), 17–49.

Introna, L.D., & Nissenbaum, H. (2000). Shaping the Web: Why the politics of search engines matters. *Information Society*, *16*(3), 169–185.

Kellogg, K.C., Valentine, M.A., & Christin, A. (2020). Algorithms at work: The new contested terrain of control. *Academy of Management Annals*, *14*(1), 366–410.

Lupton, D., & Jutel, A. (2015). 'It's like having a physician in your pocket!' A critical analysis of self-diagnosis smartphone apps. *Social Science & Medicine*, *133*, 128–135.

Manyika, J., Lund, S., Chui, M., Bughin, J., Woetzel, J., et al. (2017). *Jobs lost, jobs gained: Workforce transitions in a time of automation.* McKinsey Global Institute, 1–148.

March, J.G. (1988). Technology of foolishness. In *Decisions and organizations*, J.G. March (ed.), Oxford: Blackwell, pp. 253–265.

March, J.G., & Weil, T. (2009). *On leadership.* Hoboken, NJ: John Wiley & Sons.

Mittelstadt, B.D., Allo, P., Taddeo, M., Wachter, S., & Floridi, L. (2016). The ethics of algorithms: Mapping the debate. *Big Data and Society*, *3*(2), 1–21.

Newell, S., & Marabelli, M. (2015). Strategic opportunities (and challenges) of algorithmic decision-making: A call for action on the long-term societal effects of 'datification'. *Journal of Strategic Information Systems*, *24*(1), 3–14.

Nikolaidis, S., & Shah, J. (2012). Human–robot teaming using shared mental models. *ACM/IEEE HRI.*

OECD (2016). *Automation and independent work in a digital economy.* OECD Policy Brief on The Future of Work, Brussels.

Orlikowski, W.J., & Scott, S.V. (2016). *Digital work: A research agenda.* A Research Agenda for Management and Organization Studies. Cheltenham, UK and Northampton, MA, USA: Edward Elgar Publishing.

Pachidi, S., & Huysman, M. (2016). *Organizational intelligence in the digital age: Analytics and the cycle of choice.* Routledge Companions in Business, Management, and Accounting. London, UK and New York, USA: Routledge.

Pine, K.H., & Liboiron, M. (2015). The politics of measurement and action. In *Proceedings of the 33rd annual ACM conference on human factors in computing systems.*

Pine, K.H., & Mazmanian, M. (2017). Artful and contorted coordinating: The ramifications of imposing formal logics of task jurisdiction on situated practice. *Academy of Management Journal*, *60*(2), 720–742.

Polanyi, M. (1966). *The tacit dimension.* Garden City: Doubleday.

Sachon, M., & Boquet, I. (2017). KUKA: Planning for the Future of Automation. In *IESE Business School Case: Universidad de Navarra.*

Santiago, D., & Escrig, T. (2017). Why explainable AI must be central to responsible AI: Accenture. https://www.accenture.com/us-en/blogs/blogs-why-explainable-ai-must-central-responsible-ai.

Sergeeva, A.V., Faraj, S., & Huysman, M. (2020). Losing touch: An embodiment perspective on coordination in robotic surgery. *Organization Science*, *31*(5), 1248–1271.

Shah, J., Wiken, J., Williams, B., & Breazeal, C. (2011). Improved human–robot team performance using chaski, a human-inspired plan execution system. In *Proceedings of the 6th International Conference on Human–Robot Interaction.*

Susskind, D. (2020). *A world without work: Technology, automation, and how we should respond.* London: Allen Lane.

Zarsky, T. (2016). The trouble with algorithmic decisions: An analytic road map to examine efficiency and fairness in automated and opaque decision making. *Science, Technology, and Human Values*, *41*(1), 118–132.

4. Methods and introduction to cases

4.1 INTRODUCTION

In this chapter, we describe the research methods used to collect and analyse our eight cases and provide an introduction to each of these eight examples. This chapter describes the general characteristics of each organization and what its artificial intelligence (AI) system entails. Please note: this chapter contains only general details about the organizations and their AI systems. In the chapters that follow, we take a closer look at specific aspects of managing AI and provide further details to the cases.

4.2 RESEARCH METHODS

Across the next chapters of this book, we showcase eight different cases. As mentioned in Chapter 1, we specifically focus on incumbent organizations that have implemented AI systems into their existing work processes. The selection criteria and our aim for obtaining as much detail as possible have not always made it easy for us to gain access to organizations. Often, our requests were denied because organizations were afraid that they might disclose confidential information or lose their competitive advantage. Despite this, we found eight organizations that were willing and enthusiastic to participate in our research. These organizations provided us with detailed insights into the choices, problems and challenges they encountered along their path to manage AI in practice. Only one organization did not want to be named and is therefore anonymized in this book.

For our research, we conducted several interviews with stakeholders at each organization. In all cases, we approached the developers of the AI system, management and users. We also made use of documented material that was provided to us by the organizations or that was publicly available. Also, some organizations allowed us to conduct observations in their workplace. Using all the information collected, we developed a detailed narrative (approximately ten pages) per case. We presented these narratives to the interviewees or a contact person within the organization. Thus, we can claim that the descriptions we provide in this book are representative of the experiences of those involved.

We then analysed and coded the narratives, from which the most important and overarching themes, choices and challenges emerged. The analysis helped us to arrive at the classification of the following four chapters:

*   Organizing for data.
*   Testing and validating.
*   Algorithmic brokering.
*   Changing work.

Based on these four organizing chapters, we created a table with examples from the cases. Of course, not every case yielded detailed information on each of the four themes. We therefore used our coding process to select the strongest, most detailed parts per case related to each theme. We use these parts illustratively in the coming chapters. Not all practical cases can therefore be found in every chapter. In the following, a general introduction for each of the eight practical cases is given to provide an overview of the cases.

4.3 CASE DESCRIPTIONS

4.3.1 Helpdesk Chatbot

Centraal Beheer (CB), part of Achmea, is one of the largest and oldest insurance companies in the Netherlands. However, partially due to global digitization, the insurance industry has been under great pressure for some time now. Thus, many of these organizations were forced to change their business model and increasingly focus on providing services in addition to providing insurance. Recently, CB has expanded the range of its service offerings, and these services are increasingly based on data-driven technologies. In addition, customers are becoming more demanding and, for example, expect to receive an answer to their questions 24/7. This is why CB is now investing heavily in AI to be able to personalize its services (even more), to align itself with customer expectations, and to remain an innovative player in the market.

One of these projects is an AI-based customer service chatbot called CeeBee. CeeBee aims to answer simple customer questions. In line with customer expectations, the chatbot is available 24/7. A customer accessing the digital channels of CB can receive immediate support from the chatbot. Also, CeeBee automates some helpdesk tasks, which gives helpdesk workers more space and time to deal with more complex issues.

The latest and most mathematically complex version of CeeBee has recently been successfully implemented. Interestingly, CB has developed its chatbot technology experience over time by choosing to develop and implement the chatbot in phases: from a system with relatively few functionalities, for example having no button features, to an increasingly comprehensive version.

The first version of the chatbot – a so-called 'linear' chatbot – is developed with the help of an external chatbot software provider. In this first phase, the objective was to reduce the workload of helpdesk workers by having the chatbot answer simple questions and direct customers to email forms. The linear chatbot is a pre-programmed bot, working with pre-composed dialogues. These dialogues consist of a series of possible question–answer conversations that a customer typically performs with a helpdesk employee; for example, questions about the coverage of certain policies or how to make adjustments to an insurance contract. For the linear chatbot, these dialogues are a kind of script where customers can ask for information in all kinds of ways, and which offers various ways in which the bot can respond.

One of the challenges in using the pre-programmed chatbot provided by a third party is that it requires intensive contact between CB and the supplier. For example, each change or update has to be requested separately by CB. This is not efficient and makes it difficult to implement changes. Besides, CB's goal is to create a chatbot that is AI-driven (not script-based) and that can be used by multiple branches within Achmea. Thus, CB decided to further develop this AI-driven chatbot internally and heavily expanded its development team to three times its original size. The team equipped the existing chatbot with a smart algorithm that no longer follows a linear script, but can determine the meaning of a sentence by using machine learning (a so-called 'nonlinear' chatbot). As a result, CeeBee can now solve a wide variety of queries.

In the latest version of CeeBee, which has recently been implemented, the system is trained in all the different meanings that a particular phrase can have in a particular situation. To be able to offer the customer a solution, the algorithm had to learn the underlying question of a text by means of machine learning. For example, the AI system is trained to recognize all possible words that represent the subject or the direct object; in the sentence, 'There is damage to my car', CeeBee now recognizes the subject ('damage') and the direct object ('car'). In this way, the chatbot can 'understand' the intention behind a large number of questions and provide relevant information to the customer (see Figure 4.1 for an impression of CeeBee).

4.3.2   Predictive People Analytics

'MultiCo'[1] is one of the largest fast-moving consumer goods organizations in the world. The organization has approximately 200 000 employees in more than 50 countries worldwide and has annual sales of more than $50 billion. Every year, more than 10 000 candidates apply for the talent programmes of MultiCo Europe. To transform the method for selecting applicants, the human

Source: Centraal Beheer.

Figure 4.1   *Helpdesk chatbot CeeBee*

resources (HR) department saw an opportunity to use AI for the recruitment and selection of its talent programmes. In September 2018, the HR department of the European headquarters launched an AI system for the recruitment and selection of new employees.

MultiCo's interest in AI stems from a broader strategic initiative to innovate and prepare the HR department for the future of work by supporting HR processes with new digital technologies. Additionally, in the assessment of applicants, the HR department values objectivity and efficiency. According to MultiCo's HR manager, the AI system operationalizes these values by helping the organization to:

1. Assess applicants more objectively and fairly.
2. Provide insights into the personality traits of applicants predictive of success within the organization.
3. Empower HR professionals and managers to make objective and data-driven decisions.

The AI system in question was developed externally by a third party ('NeuroYou'[2]). Its promise was that MultiCo could make more objective, fair and efficient hiring decisions through the application of data science, neuroscience and machine learning.

The external party provided a system that can be used in the first two rounds of the talent programme selection process. In the first round, applicants are asked to play 15 online neuroscientific games, which assess concentration, emotional intelligence and leadership qualities. Based on these scores, the algorithm calculates the extent to which candidates match the profile of successful MultiCo employees.

Those who fit the desired profile then proceed to the second round: the video interview. For the video interview, the third party provided video analysis software for analysing applicants' facial expressions. Based on their expressions, applicants are screened and automatically advanced to the next round or disqualified. However, at the time of writing in summer 2020, this capability of the AI system has not (yet) been adopted by the HR professionals at MultiCo. The team has doubts about the quality of the video data used to train the algorithm and is disappointed by the predictive power of the algorithm, since the algorithm's predictions hardly match the human assessments of the HR professionals.

On the contrary, the AI system using neuroscientific games is now also in use at MultiCo's global headquarters in the United States and has been evaluated as a success by the organization. Within the European headquarters, the AI system has also been used for recruitment and selection of general functions in sales and information technology (IT) since 2019. To date, however, the system is not used as an automatic selection tool, but rather as an informative tool. Also, in 2020, new discussions started about the use of the automatic video analysis software. The AI system is therefore both in full use and still in development.

4.3.3 Consumption Prediction

KLM Royal Dutch Airlines (hereafter, 'KLM') has an average annual turnover of €10 billion, 33 000 employees, and 100 years of experience in the airline industry. However, of course the organization still has to continue to develop to make work processes as efficient and flexible as possible. That is why KLM is now putting significant energy into developing AI systems by looking at how they can be created and used to solve complex operational issues and facilitate decision-making in diverse areas. For the development of AI systems within and outside KLM, it has entered into a partnership with the Boston Consulting Group.

One of the main challenges for KLM is to create a technical environment to enable an integrated approach to the control of operational processes. Within airlines, various departments often exist in silos. By taking an integrated approach, the intention is to bypass the 'nuisance' of department boundaries. Important conditions for such an approach are that there must be key performance indicators and that the processes must be digitized as much as possible. Therefore, a substantial part of the IT investments at KLM in recent years has focused on unlocking data from existing systems, to create optimization tools, and develop machine learning models. 'Front-line staff tools' is one of the categories of systems for which machine learning is applied. These enable operations employees to make better decisions and improve customer service.

One of the front-line staff systems that has since been developed is the Meals-on-Board System (MOBS). MOBS is a supervised learning algorithm created internally by KLM at the start of 2018. It aims to increase the efficiency of catering orders that are loaded on board before aircraft departure. The system predicts how many passengers with a ticket will be on board the aircraft. The forecasts start 17 days in advance and then are adjusted 7, 4, 3, 2 and 1 day to even a few hours in advance. Both booking and flight data are used for MOBS. This data includes information about whether or not someone is a frequent traveller, whether it is a business or leisure flight, the connection time between a transfer, the destination, business or economy class, and aircraft capacity.

By using MOBS, the catering order is better linked to how many meals are needed on board. In addition, the use of this AI system ensures that some of the decisions made by the catering department become automated. This gives the ground crew additional time to solve more complex, sometimes last-minute issues. Since the application of MOBS, KLM has been able to reduce food waste on both European and intercontinental flights by an average of 50 per cent compared to previously.

4.3.4   Predictive Policing

The Dutch National Police Force (hereafter, 'police') is the umbrella term for all 26 police forces in the Netherlands. The organization has a total of almost 64 000 employees, spread over 168 police stations. Unfortunately, the police have been struggling with a capacity decline for years. There are several reasons for this, but persistent cutbacks and retirement of the baby boom generation of policemen – who will collectively retire in the coming years – are mentioned as the two most important reasons. As a result of these persistent capacity problems, the police have increasingly focused on finding alternative options for scheduling and deploying employees as efficiently as possible.

Internationally, with the United States (US) in the lead, work has been ongoing since 2008 to use AI to schedule and deploy officers, which is called 'predictive policing'. One of the most important examples is the US version PredPol,[3] which is used to predict when and where certain patterned types of crime may take place (such as home or car burglaries, or public nuisance). In 2012, the Dutch police set up a project group to investigate whether such a predictive AI system could also be introduced in the Netherlands.

However, such systems are not undisputed. For example, the media claims that such systems can lead to a kind of self-fulfilling prophecy. By carrying out targeted actions at locations where the risk of crime is highest, the police automatically register more crime at those locations. Though crime is not necessarily higher in those locations versus others, when officers are there at that particular place and time (and not elsewhere), this is where data is gathered, which is then recorded in the database and becomes the basis of new predictions. In this way, a location can become designated as a troubling area through this vicious cycle of prediction. Another common argument is that such systems hide the profiling (for example, due to ethnicity) of certain groups even more, because the data used for such systems is not neutral, but contains prejudices that have been ingrained in police work for decades.

Partially due to these warnings, the Dutch police hired a data scientist in 2012 to start working in a project group aimed at creating a predictive AI system that would be less sensitive to the above-mentioned criticisms. In 2013, the first version of the internally developed Crime Anticipation System (CAS) was tested in daily use. This first version contained a neural network, but this was later changed to a much simpler, logistic regression due to the limited server capacity of the police. Using a neural network, it takes 20 minutes of computing time per police station per week to arrive at results. If CAS were to be implemented nationwide across 168 police stations, it would take at least 56 hours to calculate the results. This took too long, so an alternative solution was sought.

Since the police's servers could not be adapted in the short term, the project group decided to abandon the neural network and use logistic regression instead in combination with supervised learning. To predict where and when crime will happen in a week, the variable 'incident versus no incident' is related to approximately 55 predictors such as previous crimes, average household income and household size. According to calculations, this result is just as accurate and takes only one-twentieth of the computation time of the neural network.

To this day, CAS predicts a week in advance where (per $125m^2$ block) and when (per four hour block) the chances for pattern-based crime are greatest (see Figure 4.2 for an example of CAS location blocks). CAS is now used in almost all 168 police stations throughout the Netherlands.

4.3.5   Predictive Tumour Modelling

The Leiden University Medical Center (LUMC) is an academic hospital. It first opened its doors in 1873, and since then it has grown into a centre with about 7000 employees. The LUMC focuses not only on providing day-to-day care within the hospital with various specializations, but also on medical and biomedical training, as well as medical scientific research.

In recent years, medical institutes have seen a shift from traditional healthcare toward value-based healthcare (VBHC). Performing hospital tasks

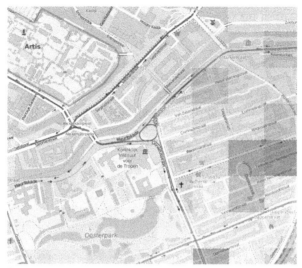

Source: https://www.politieacademie.nl/kennisenonderzoek/kennis/mediatheek/PDF/93263.PDF.

Figure 4.2   *CAS map*

involves both maximizing the quality of care for the patient and reducing the costs of care. VBHC is accompanied by major organizational changes at the hospital level. Partly due to the institutional shifts towards VBHC, the LUMC started in June 2019 with a change in its strategy: LUMC 2.0, a multidisciplinary project for health innovation within the hospital. LUMC 2.0 is a project with broad ambitions towards e-health and IT, with sub-projects such as data-driven treatments, responsible AI, cloud platforms and the implementation of a new IT architecture.

In the long term, LUMC 2.0 is expected to have major consequences, especially for radiologists. After all, radiologists are often frontrunners when it comes to technological innovation. For example, the X-ray was the innovation that started the profession. Also, radiology has become almost completely digitized in the past ten years. The X-rays that were previously developed by hand and hung on a lightbox are now digitally produced, reported and archived. These developments have also resulted in the availability of large amounts of digital images within the radiology department. The result is that imaging now plays a central role in healthcare. The increase in the amount of digital imaging available and the corresponding demand for quantitative analysis of these images means that there is a growing demand for automation. Thus, the availability of large amounts of digital data is now critical for developing

AI systems to automate radiological tasks, such as image review and image processing support.

Of course, the LUMC did not just randomly start developing learning algorithms to automate image processing. Instead, it decided to specifically focus on 'profit' maximization areas using the VBHC principle, maximizing the quality of patient care while minimizing costs. After careful consideration, it turned out that the tasks that radiologists perform around the treatment of a vestibular schwannoma (VS) are best qualified. A VS is a benign tumour that grows slowly within the skull. Despite being a benign tumour, the slow but continued growth of a VS can put pressure on the nerves and brainstem, causing symptoms such as hearing loss, dizziness, balance problems and facial paralysis.

There are two reasons for the LUMC to develop an AI system for analysing VS. Firstly, despite the slow-growing VS, many time-consuming follow-up examinations are required. An algorithm that can predict the growth rate of VS is of added value to avoid unnecessary follow-up examinations, thus avoiding unnecessary healthcare costs and patient discomfort. Secondly, the volume of the tumour can be accurately measured in three dimensions (3D), a task that takes a lot of time for radiologists and which normally results in variations of up to 40 per cent between different radiologists.

Thus, developing an AI system that can automate and standardize VS measurements can lead to higher efficiency and more consistent tumour evaluation. These reasons were convincing for hospital management, and in October 2019, the LUMC started internally developing an AI system with supervised learning that serves two purposes. Firstly, it can automatically process magnetic resonance imaging (MRI) scans, segment the VS tumours, and calculate the volume of tumours. Second, a predictive model for the development of VS is generated, based on scans and clinical information from the ear, nose and throat (ENT) department. This way, scans can be performed more efficiently, taking time-consuming tasks off the hands of radiologists, and making follow-up treatments for patients faster and more personalized.

4.3.6   Smart Powerplants

Volkswagen was founded in Wolfsburg, Germany in 1937. Today, Volkswagen AG is the parent company of the Volkswagen Group, which consists of 12 different brands, with 122 factories all over the world, and approximately 656 000 employees. In 2015, Volkswagen gained negative attention when 'diesel-gate' came to light. In short, Volkswagen was accused of finding a 'creative' way to pass emissions tests in both the United States and Europe, while the cars' carbon dioxide (CO_2) emissions in daily use were about 40 times more than the official allowance.

In response to this negative publicity, in 2016, Volkswagen published the TOGETHER Strategy 2025 and outlined its plan to become the most sustainable car manufacturer in the world by 2025. Part of this strategy is a strong focus on innovation, which should contribute to Volkswagen's sustainability policy of four points:

1. Climate change: by 2050, Volkswagen must become a CO_2-neutral organization.
2. Air quality: by 2030, 40 per cent of passenger cars must run on electricity.
3. Environmental compliance: Volkswagen wants to become a role model in environmentally friendly manufacturing.
4. Means of production: by 2025 there must be a 45 per cent reduction in production waste.

As a result of this renewed strong focus on innovation, a research group was set up within Volkswagen in 2016 to conduct fundamental research into machine learning.[4] Because Volkswagen wants to give the Machine Learning Research Lab researchers the space to develop ideas based on their scientific interest, only 20 per cent of the output needs to be practically relevant. This means that the development of AI systems within the Machine Learning Research Lab often arise from the personal or academic interests of researchers, and only sometimes from questions or problems of domain experts.

This is also the case regarding the 'smart powerplants', a supervised learning algorithm for determining when and on what percentage factory generators should run. In developing this system, the data scientists were interested in figuring out whether and how they could use machine learning to run the generators in a more climate-friendly way.

Within Volkswagen it is common knowledge that the deployment of generators is still planned based on rigid calendar schedules. The data scientists therefore set to work in 2016 to develop a machine learning application that can make a dynamic analysis based on, among other things, the time of the year and the output of the factory. The aim is to create a system that can make better suggestions about the use of the generators. Although this is not yet the case, those suggestions could eventually completely automate the deployment of generators. The system developed by the data scientists is estimated to be able to reduce emissions from the factories by 20 per cent.

4.3.7 Social Robotics

Philadelphia supports people with mental disabilities throughout the Netherlands and aims to empower clients to get the best out of themselves. They look at the possibilities and opportunities of the people who live in one of their care facilities, who receive intensive care or ambulatory support, but also those who come for a day to learn to spend their day meaningfully and thus discover more of their talents. For example, they help such clients develop or learn how to work and find a job. Philadelphia currently supports approximately 8600 people with disabilities and their care professionals provide tailor-made support across more than 500 small-scale locations. Philadelphia has a lot of in-house expertise, such as behavioural experts, physiotherapists, speech therapists and occupational therapists.

In 2016, Philadelphia began exploring the use of a social robot to provide support to clients. Two main reasons drive this exploration. Firstly, Philadelphia is known as an innovative organization, seeking out creative and innovative methods to deliver future care and services. To illustrate this, one of the informants said:

> When Philadelphia was founded in 1961, parents wanted to care for their children with disabilities within the neighborhood, on a small scale. However, the entire healthcare system was set up around large-scale institutions disconnected from where people live. This required developing new forms of care, taking a creative approach to obtain resources, and a great deal of perseverance to be able to take this step together with the government. Fortunately, we were met with success. Our care is still small-scale, close by, and we still listen to parents and relatives in shaping the care process.

In recent years, however, the small-scale model that distinguished Philadelphia has come under increasing pressure due to the increased need for care. This links to the second central reason for exploring the use of social robots, as the number of vulnerable people in society has been steadily increasing, while the number of healthcare professionals is declining. In addition, clients with disabilities and their families are ageing, which means that their family members, who often also play a major role in the care for these clients, will at some point lose the ability to help. As a result, Philadelphia is now developing and implementing social robot Phi in the hope that clients will be able to live independently for longer and that healthcare professionals will experience less pressure at work.

Phi is a Pepper robot, whose hardware is developed externally by a Japanese manufacturer. Pepper is an android robot that can move its head and arms and is equipped with wheels enabling it to move slowly around a room. Philadelphia has provided the robot with a facial recognition system with the aim that the robot will only initiate a conversation when it is more than 50 per cent certain of a person's identity. People can respond to the robot by entering their answer via a tablet screen attached to the robot's front (see Figure 4.3). Philadelphia is developing the software for Phi together with a partner – The Innovation Playground – so that it can make Phi meet the needs of its specific

Source: https://www.philadelphia.nl/robotica.

Figure 4.3   Social robot Phi

target group. The collaboration with The Innovation Playground resulted in the startup Robot Ctrl, which is the platform from which Phi is controlled and on which its interactions are programmed. For example, it is working on improving Phi's AI system for facial recognition, so that Phi will soon be able to recognize individuals under various lighting conditions. Especially regarding Phi's interaction with humans, much can be gained with AI techniques, such as the application of natural language processing (NLP).

Phi is thus still in full development, but Phi is also already being used in practice. Philadelphia has set up a multi-year programme that allows it to continue researching and developing the robot in use, through robot 'overnights' with clients.

4.3.8   Money Laundering Prediction

ABN AMRO is a large Dutch bank with approximately 18 000 employees and a history that goes back to the 19th century. Though the typical activities that first come to mind when thinking about a bank are, for example, bringing lenders and borrowers together, providing financial advice and arranging payments, societal engagement by the financial sector has become increasingly important over the years. For example, the financial sector is playing an increasingly important role in the fight against financial crime. The Dutch Prevention of Money Laundering and Terrorist Financing Act has been in force since 2008, giving financial institutions, and in particular banks, a gatekeeper role.

They thus have a responsibility to prevent, detect and report money laundering and terrorist financing within their infrastructure. According to ABN AMRO's website,[5] worldwide criminal transactions account for around €2400 billion a year, including money laundering and financing terrorism. In the Netherlands, 6.6 billion transactions are carried out per year, of which a very small percentage is illegal. Detecting these suspicious transactions is therefore like looking for a needle in a haystack: taking a lot of time and requiring very precise work. ABN AMRO therefore increasingly uses technological means combined with more than 2400 human analysts to fulfil its responsibilities as a gatekeeper.

One of the most recent examples specifically aims at anti-money laundering and is called the 'anti-money laundering' (AML) system; an AI system that can generate targeted potential laundering alerts based on which analysts can then determine whether or not a transaction is appropriate. The primary purpose of using this AI system is to increase the effectiveness of detecting suspicious transactions. This is done by improving the quality of existing alerts and by supplementing these with new types of alerts for which human pattern recognition capabilities are limited.

ABN AMRO is developing internally supervised and unsupervised models for this purpose from 2019, based on open-source algorithms. The supervised model improves the quality of the existing alerts because the model is trained on data about when alerts are reported. The unsupervised model is a type of anomaly detection model: a model aimed at detecting outliers or rare actions. This unsupervised model must discover new patterns in the data to surface the previously unseen and therefore unknown. The AI system was used in a test environment in the first quarter of 2020, after which, in the spring of 2020, it has been implemented into the daily work of analysts.

4.4   SUMMARY

The eight cases that we have described above provide broad insight into the current state of AI in different organizations and within different sectors. Table 4.1 provides an overview of the characteristics of each of the eight examples. In the next four chapters, we will use and further elaborate on these real-life examples to discuss what managing AI means in practice.

Table 4.1   *Overview of specifics of cases*

Organization	AI system	AI technique	Development	Reasons for development	Current status
CB	Helpdesk chatbot, CeeBee	1. Linear chatbot 2. NLP enabled nonlinear chatbot	1. External 2. Internal	• Reduce workload • Increase efficiency • Part of a broader strategic initiative	1. Retired 2. In use
MultiCo	Predictive people analytics	1. Neuroscientific games with supervised learning 2. Video analysis with image recognition	External with internal guidance	• More objective decisions • Better overview of applicants • Part of a broader strategic initiative	1. In use 2. Rejected; new conversations in progress
KLM	Meals-on-Board System, MOBS	Supervised learning	Internal	• Expensive and externally managed IT system • Reduced weight on board airplanes • Part of a broader strategic initiative	In use
Police	Predictive policing, CAS	Supervised learning	Internal	• Growing capacity problems • More objective decisions • Part of a broader strategic initiative	In use
LUMC	Predictive tumour modelling	Supervised learning for image review and processing	Internal	• Increase efficiency • More consistent diagnoses • Part of a broader strategic initiative	Being implemented
Volkswagen	Smart powerplants	Supervised learning	Internal	• Overarching social problem • Personal interest of researchers • Part of a broader strategic initiative	In use

Organization	AI system	AI technique	Development	Reasons for development	Current status
Philadelphia	Social robot, Phi	Supervised learning for: 1. Face recognition 2. Natural language processing	1. External/ internal 2. Internal	• Less pressure on healthcare professionals • Enable patients to live independently for longer • Part of a broader strategic initiative	1. In use 2. In development
ABN AMRO	Anti money laundering (AML) system	1. Supervised learning for known patterns 2. Unsupervised learning for new patterns	Internal	• Greater institutional pressure to find solutions to, e.g., track money laundering practices • Labour-intensive existing methods	In use

NOTES

1. Pseudonym, the name of the organization in question remains anonymous for privacy reasons.
2. Pseudonym, the name of the developer remains anonymous for privacy reasons.
3. PredPol was introduced in 2008 by the Los Angeles Police Department.
4. https://www.argmax.ai/blog/about/.
5. https://careers.abnamro.com/go/Detecting-Financial-Crime/8121000/.

5. Organizing for data

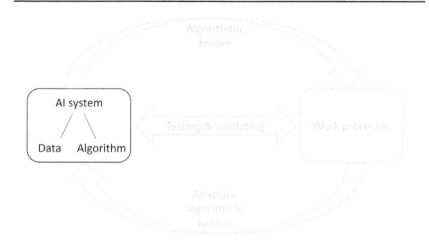

Figure 5.0   *Overview of core themes: Chapter 5*

5.1   INTRODUCTION

In this chapter, we discuss one of the central building blocks of artificial intelligence (AI): data. Much is written about the extensive digitization and datafication of organizational processes (e.g., Davenport et al., 2012; Faraj et al., 2018; McAfee et al., 2012, O'Neil, 2016; Von Krogh, 2018; Zuboff, 2019). This may lead to a managerial assumption that, when an AI system is being developed or needs to be developed, data is already available. Yet, the examples in this book show that this is far from the case.

In Chapter 2, we described the great ambitions for the development of artificial general intelligence, which is intended to be able to perform a variety of tasks. In practice, however, this is still a long way off. At this point, AI systems are very narrow, aimed at performing a specific task (for example, predicting a specific type of criminal incidents, or detecting a specific type of tumour). In order to perform such a task, an AI system should be developed specifically for that task. This is not just about choosing the correct or most appropriate mathematical approach (the algorithm), which is often the job of the developer; the data used to create and train the system is also critical to the operation of the system. The better the data connects to the task the AI system has to perform, the more accurately the system can do its job.

So-called Big Data strategies, which have been largely adopted by organizations in recent years, are now also being examined critically. The 'garbage in, garbage out' argument – that is, if you enter data of low quality into the system, it will produce poor outcomes – is increasingly associated with these types of large, unstructured datasets. Such datasets have to be cleaned up, which takes a tremendous amount of work, and what subsequently remains as usable data is surprisingly meagre (Di Russo, 2020). Using these big datasets is thus not always sufficient to create an effective AI system that seamlessly connects to organizational processes. An AI system should, in the words of data scientists, be 'fed' with the correct, organization- or task-specific data, and this data should be created, collected and delivered from within the organization. An important first part of managing AI is therefore organizing for data.

In this chapter, we will discuss what 'organizing for data' exactly means. Because large amounts of appropriate data to train the learning algorithms is a requirement that is unique to AI systems – we have not seen this at such magnitude in previous technologies – this may have a major impact on how organizations set up their work processes (see also Chapter 2 on how an AI system learns through data). Our cases demonstrate that employees sometimes have to (temporarily) perform new tasks to generate the data needed to create and train the AI system. Additionally, some organizations choose to develop new positions that focus specifically on creating data, to spare the existing employees or because creating a specific dataset is highly specialized work. We give an example of both options.

Our cases also demonstrate that the new tasks and responsibilities that arise in relation to organizing for data can help to stay involved in and knowledgeable of the development of the algorithm. We provide an example of this. This chapter concludes with a look at the challenges related to organizing for data.

5.2   ORGANIZING FOR DATA IN PRACTICE

In this section, the cases MultiCo and Philadelphia address the process of data construction and provide insight into what it means if data has to be delivered from within the organization. CB and the LUMC highlight how some organizations choose to create a new role (or a whole new group) that bears the responsibility for data collection and construction. To conclude, MultiCo illustrates how new data skills and responsibilities can also help to stay involved in and knowledgeable of the development of the algorithm.

5.2.1   The Process of Data Construction

At the beginning of this chapter, we stated that a lot of attention has been paid to Big Data in recent years. The presence of such datasets is often cited as the reason why AI systems should be implemented in organizations, because AI systems need to extract 'value' from that data (e.g., Di Russo, 2020; Hartmann and Henkel, 2020). We briefly discussed the current criticism regarding these general, unstructured datasets. The cases in this section highlight the central role of internally collected data for the development of AI systems and for connecting these to existing work processes.

The cases MultiCo and Philadelphia show the laboriousness and complexity of this process. In the case of MultiCo, the AI system is developed externally, but the data is created internally and collected by the employees. This data is then used directly for training an AI system. At Philadelphia, the data created and collected has multiple purposes: to allow the AI system to learn, and to further develop as an organization.

MultiCo: predictive people analytics
MultiCo has chosen to have the AI system for recruitment and selection developed externally (see Chapter 4). This developer, here referred to as 'NeuroYou',[1] has extensive experience in providing neuroscientific tools to map the characteristics and skills of applicants and employees. NeuroYou does, however, encourage MultiCo to provide the data that should be used to train and further develop the AI system, because it believes that if the algorithm is trained using data about MultiCo's own employees, it is better able to make accurate predictions about its applicants.

MultiCo's managers agree to provide internal data and in order to generate this the human resources (HR) professionals approach 300 employees, asking them to play online games based on neuroscientific insights. The games are used to measure character traits such as their ability to concentrate, emotional intelligence and leadership qualities. In addition, the employees record a video interview, allowing image analysis software to also be trained on the data of the internal employees. By letting the employees play these online games, the external developers thus gain access to data of 300 internal employees which can be used to specifically train its algorithms.

Along with the efforts of the employees, the HR professionals also provide performance data (that is, data on how well each employee performs) on the 300 employees to NeuroYou. In this way, scores for the online games and the characteristics in the video interview can be linked to the performance of the employees, which makes it possible to measure which scores are achieved by successful employees. The profile of the successful employees is then used to calculate to what extent the scores of an applicant correspond to this. Accordingly, based on supervised learning and data on MultiCo's own employees, NeuroYou develops a predictive model about which applicants should and should not be hired.

However, creating a dataset on which the learning algorithm can be trained is not an easy task for HR professionals and involves new responsibilities. First of all, as discussed above, they are responsible for selecting employees in order to collect the relevant data for training the algorithm. In this process, the HR professionals – as 'experts' regarding the employees and the type of work they perform – must make important decisions about the selection of employees and the performance indicators utilized to collect data. Because the selection of employees should represent the organization, this new responsibility for HR professionals also requires new knowledge about data requirements, such as sample selection and data quantity and quality, and an understanding of new data legislation, such as the General Data Protection Regulation (GDPR). To support HR professionals in obtaining this new knowledge, MultiCo facilitates training courses focused on data and statistics.

A consequence of the active role of the HR professionals in gathering data is that in the data analysis phase they are actively involved in discussions about whether or not to include variables that, according to the algorithm, predict success in the organization. In order to align the AI system with MultiCo's work processes, HR professionals are given the freedom and responsibility to include or exclude certain variables in the AI system of the online games. For example, the first results of the AI system show that 'attaching little value to working conditions' can be a significant predictor of a successful employee. According to the HR professionals, this outcome does not fit with MultiCo's work processes, because it could mean that new applicants are selected while they do not care about good working conditions. This type of employee does not match what the HR team considers to be a good employee. In the data analysis phase, the HR professionals therefore decide not to include this variable in the algorithm. As a result of the new responsibilities, the HR professionals thus have a direct influence on the final decision model for selecting applicants. We will discuss this in more detail in section 5.2.3.

Philadelphia: social robotics
At Philadelphia, organizing for the data required for the development of social robot Phi is also a complex and time-consuming process. Naturally, it wants to use the data in innovative ways, but the data that is collected generally concerns the provision of care to vulnerable persons, which makes it extra important that the collected data is handled responsibly. When Philadelphia decided to start working with social robots in 2016, little practical research had been done on this, and almost nothing was known about how social robots could be used for care and services. For example, there was little knowledge about the responses

social robots might elicit in clients. That is why Philadelphia decided to design the first phase of the commissioning of the social robot Phi as an experiment. It focuses on collecting data for both machine learning (interaction data) and organizational learning (for example, how different clients react to the robots during a so-called 'sleepover').

Before the robot is deployed for a first stay with a client, the Philadelphia robot team (which includes developers and healthcare professionals) conducts various conversations with the client and their family and caregivers. Here, development goals, whereby the robot should offer support, are determined. During these conversations, data is collected about the life of the client, such as habits and needs. The development goals, programming what Phi has to do to achieve them, how the client responds to this, and the interaction content between Phi and the client, are used to further develop the AI systems.

During the first robot stay of two to three weeks, data is collected regarding the interaction between the client and the robot. In this way, a database is built from which Phi's 'speech' can be automated in small steps. As one of the informants explains:

> We have to do everything now ... we have to pre-assemble and program every minute of every day; there is of course also a lot of repetition, but creating the interaction content and conversation content ... is incredibly intensive. It is also not possible without humans, but AI should help us as soon as possible.

However, automating the interaction content is not the most important thing for Philadelphia. Much more important is that it knows for sure that Phi does not make mistakes (meaning that the quality of the interaction content should be optimal). Given the target group of Phi, careful development and testing of the interaction content is of primary importance. We will discuss this in more detail in Chapter 6.

In addition to collecting data for applying machine learning for interaction content, Philadelphia also collects data for organizational learning. This concerns data on, for instance, how clients deal with Phi, which is collected through home visits and personal contact between the robot team and the client. Philadelphia wants to understand how different clients with different care needs deal differently with the robot, but in order to learn from the interactions, behaving as normally as possible during the robot stay is also important. The collected data is therefore now still limited to conversations and observations about the type and quality of interactions. Because Phi can be controlled online, the robot team can also collect data about when Phi is used and the duration of use. This gives them a better idea of how the interaction with Phi develops over a certain period of time. The purpose of the data that is collected here is not so much to allow the AI system to learn, but to learn from it as an organization, so that the robot stays can be used as optimally as possible in the work process. In Chapter 6, we elaborate on how the work processes at Philadelphia are included in the testing and validation of the AI system.

Both MultiCo and Philadelphia provide insight into the laboriousness and complexity of the data construction process, which is necessary for the proper alignment of an AI system in practice. At MultiCo, the collected data is used directly by the developers to train the externally developed AI system, so that it meets the needs of the organization as closely as possible. Data collection at Philadelphia has two purposes. On the one hand, machine learning techniques should be applied to automate the interaction of Phi with clients. In addition, the robot team collects data with the aim of being able to learn from this as an organization, and to adapt the robot stays accordingly. Collecting data at Philadelphia therefore also has an organizational learning aspect, which can benefit work processes. With both examples, we emphasize that in order to develop an effective AI system, organizing extensive, internally oriented data collection is necessary.

5.2.2   New Roles for Data Construction

In this section, we discuss – on the basis of the cases CB and the LUMC – that a new role can be made available to transform data construction from an afterthought into a main task. At CB the new position of 'conversation specialist' is established due to the specialized nature of conversation data that should be created to develop an AI-based chatbot. A separate department has been set up at the LUMC to relieve radiologists of the time-consuming work required to create and maintain datasets.

CB: helpdesk chatbot
CB has opted to develop and implement its chatbot CeeBee in phases (see Chapter 4). The most important data for the development of the first, linear chatbot consists of pre-composed dialogues. These dialogues consist of a series of possible question–answer conversations that a customer could have with a helpdesk agent. For the linear chatbot, the dialogues reflect a kind of script that simulates a large number of formats in which customers can request information.

Because CB offers insurance and (financial) services, the dialogues often consist of questions about the coverage of certain insurances or requests to change or amend a contract. The dialogues are based on conversations that helpdesk employees have with customers. In order to develop these dialogues, CB has made a new position available: the so-called conversation specialist. At the time of the development of the linear chatbot, creating dialogues was their core task. Ultimately, more than 300 different dialogues were developed by the conversation specialists.

With the further developments towards the new AI-based chatbot, such conversation data has remained important. In fact, it has become even more essential. With this 'smarter' version of the chatbot, however, a specific script for a question–answer conversation is no longer followed in a linear fashion. Instead, the dialogues are used to train the AI system to conduct an unprogrammed question–answer conversation itself. The AI system does not remember a limited number of pre-programmed sentences, but learns to find out the meaning of a sentence. This means that the system has to be trained in all the different meanings that a sentence can have in a particular situation. This is done by training the system to find out the underlying question in a text. For example, for the sentence 'There is damage to my car', the AI system should learn to recognize that 'damage' is the subject and 'car' is the direct object. In order to understand the intention behind a question – and to be able to provide an answer relevant to the customer – the chatbot is trained to recognize all possible words that have to do with the subject or the direct object.

To train the AI system, the developers can still use the dialogues that were initially developed for the linear system, as these represent customer conversations. Interestingly enough, the role of the conversation specialist has grown with the development of the AI system and has only become more important. More specifically, they have changed from 'traditional' communication experts to the role of conversational designer. The conversational designer creates dialogues and then tests whether these have been correctly translated into the AI system. Here, the conversational designer looks at whether the AI system provides answers that correspond to the thought-out conversation. The conversation specialists now teach the AI system to speak, as it were, by checking, for instance, whether the chatbot has indeed extracted the correct meaning from a sentence. Given the almost unlimited number of nuances a language can contain; it still proves to be quite a challenge to teach the chatbot to speak.

LUMC: predictive tumour modelling
The development process of the AI system for analysing a vestibular schwannoma (VS) at the LUMC starts with the collection, integration and export of data. Because the AI model should be trained to generalize for different tumour sizes and types, strict selection criteria are used to construct a diversified dataset (for example, different types and sizes of VS tumours). In addition, the data should be of high quality with, for example, sufficient image quality and the same scanning protocols.

For this data project, the Radiology department chooses to deploy two non-radiologists as observers so that this does not become yet another responsibility of the radiologists. The main task of these two observers is to analyse magnetic resonance imaging (MRI) scans of patients with a VS, drawing contours around the tumour. This data is then used to train the AI system. The two observers perform work that is part of a new group created by the LUMC: the Imaging Services Group. A logical consequence of the ISG is that it facilitates the development and implementation of AI. The ISG was launched in September 2018 with eight medical imaging and radiation experts and one technical physician. Together, they have expertise in both the clinical and the technical aspects of medical image processing.

Although both observers have a clinical background – a technical physician and an assistant physician from the ear, nose and throat (ENT) department – they are not trained radiologists, who are the intended users of the system. They are selected to provide training data, however, because a considerable investment of time is required to generate this training data. In addition, the handling of the required software is a specialist task. Radiologists are also relatively expensive, and due to their busy work schedule, availability is limited. As the manager of the ISG explains:

> In a perfect world, you would of course engage someone with thirty years of experience [within a certain clinical specialism]. But these [radiologists] don't have much time. So therefore, what they usually do is to let a junior handle this. And they can do it with a certain degree of accuracy. When in doubt, i.e., when a very difficult case comes along and there is uncertainty, a supervisor comes in, and that would be [radiologist #1] and [radiologist #2], and they answer the question.

The observers were trained for annotation by an experienced neuroradiologist. For this, they had a short demonstration session of about 30 minutes, and were assigned ten cases which they could work on for a longer period of time. After a few weeks, they met with the neuroradiologist to review each case. Since then, the two observers have been working unsupervised. An additional measure to guarantee the quality of the annotations is that when the difference between the two observers is greater than 10 per cent, a neuroradiologist assesses the case and makes the final judgement.

In order to minimize the burden on the full schedule of the radiologists, the LUMC has thus chosen not only to create a new role, but also to make a completely new group available for doing data-related work. Among other things, this group deals with the tasks required for the development of AI systems and gradually takes over tasks that do not necessarily have to be performed by radiologists.

CB and the LUMC provide insight into an alternative solution when it is not possible for the developer or the user to collect data. CB demonstrates how a new role can be deployed when the required properties of the datasets are too complex or specialized for the user to create. CB shows not only that data collection and construction becomes a main task in this case, but also that the expertise gained with regard to data will be used in the further development of AI. The example of the LUMC illustrates that even a new group can be used to perform data work, so that the intended user remains free to perform domain-dependent, specialized tasks. By creating a specific role, or even making a group or department available, organizing for data can therefore require taking responsibility away from developers or users and moving it to a third party. However, whether the responsibility lies with the developer, the user or a third party, in each of these cases it is important to consider whether this is done responsibly, which we will now discuss further.

5.2.3   From Data to Algorithm

More and more aspects of our behaviour can be converted into data. Combining all that data can lead to far-reaching insights into behavioural patterns, and with that to increasingly accurate and better-fitting AI systems. Fortunately, as a society, we have decided that we should not just let that happen. Instead, organizations are increasingly made aware of the need to be mindful of what happens to data and how it is translated into an algorithm. In this section, we explore the example of MultiCo. Here, the organization has chosen to engage the HR professionals as an ethical watchdog. Although the AI system is developed externally, the organization still retains internal control over the ethical considerations of what is and what is not included in the AI system, and which data is and is not used to train the algorithm. MultiCo thus provides an example of how an organization can go from organizing for data to being involved in the development of the algorithm.

MultiCo: predictive people analytics
MultiCo's HR professionals are actively involved in the collection and selection of data required to develop the algorithm for automatically selecting candidates. For them, this includes new data activities and requires new knowledge about data requirements, such as sample selection and data quantity and quality, and an understanding of new data legislation such as the GDPR.

However, the responsibility of MultiCo's HR professionals does not end there. Given the potentially major impact of the AI system on the selection of candidates, MultiCo has decided to involve the HR professionals, with their knowledge of the collected data, in the further development of the algorithm by NeuroYou. In this regard, MultiCo has taken the position that ethical guidelines should not be formulated along the margins, but should be continuously and critically reviewed during the process of AI development. The HR professionals have therefore been given the role of ethical watchdog. They continue to hold this role even now that the AI system is being developed for other departments.

In its role as ethical watchdog, the HR team has also been faced with important choices about the decision-making model of the algorithm, for instance with regard to what variables or indicators should be included or excluded. An example of this is, the indicator 'does (not) value working conditions'. According to the algorithm, not attaching value to working conditions is an indicator of a successful employee. Despite the fact that they collected the data themselves, the HR professionals do not agree with this and have decided to remove the indicator.

Another example is the ethical challenge faced in adapting the AI system for recruitment roles within sales. Initial analysis of the data reveals that a number of predictive variables play out differently depending on gender and age. More specifically, the algorithm indicates that daring to take risks is a significant predictor of success within the organization, but that women take significantly less risks than men. If they use this data to train the algorithm, it could lead to the decision model selecting mostly male applicants. HR professionals are therefore confronted with a dilemma: are they allowed and willing to select applicants on the basis of data and variables that have shown major differences between men and women in the past? And on top of this, sharing this dilemma with sales managers reveals that managers are only interested in success, regardless of exclusion of certain demographic groups. Nonetheless, the HR professionals, in their role as ethical watchdog, decided to put a stop to this. Based on the findings, they have decided not to use the algorithm at all as a selection tool for applicants for sales positions for the time being.

In order to make the step – from merely collecting data to thinking critically about the decision model – possible for HR professionals, the developers of NeuroYou organize various meetings with MultiCo's HR professionals. In these meetings, the developers present and explain the analysis techniques. In addition, they show those variables that the algorithm designates as 'predictive', that is, the traits and skills that distinguish the successful from the unsuccessful employees. These meetings are essential for the developers to be able to explain the AI system and the predictions to the HR professionals. Yet, the HR professionals decided over time – due to their involvement and responsibility regarding the ethical aspects – that a mere explanation is not enough to assess the model. For instance, they criticize the transparency of the data used. Initially, the HR professionals collect the data; however, as it is then supplied to the external developers, they lose oversight of what is and what is not used by the developers to train the algorithm. In order to perform their role as an ethical watchdog, the HR professionals – following the notion that it promotes collaboration and transparency of the development process – request and receive access to the dataset used.

The case of MultiCo demonstrates how it is possible to move from organizing for data to involvement in the development of an algorithm. At MultiCo, responsibility for ethical considerations has mainly been given to HR professionals, who have seen part of their work and responsibilities change because they have taken on the role of ethical watchdog. The new knowledge that the HR professionals have gained with regard to data collection and selection has also led to other demands with regard to the developers' work. For example, the HR professionals asked the developers to share the dataset in order to promote transparency in the development process. The new data knowledge and skills of the HR professionals are therefore used in the organization not only to collect data, but also to critically look at the development of the algorithm.

5.3 THE CHALLENGES OF ORGANIZING FOR DATA

In section 5.2, based on our cases, we provided examples of what it can mean for organizations to organize for data. We discussed the actions that organizations can take with regard to data construction, the fact that organizations can choose to make new positions available for this, and what it actually means for an organization to responsibly organize for data. In this section we go one step further. We make use of both our real-life cases and existing (popular) scientific literature, and describe three challenges to consider when organizing for data:

1. What is needed for creating data?
2. Should you buy an externally developed system or should you develop it internally?
3. How do you ensure that data specialists can collaborate with organizations?

5.3.1 Challenge 1: What is Needed for Creating Data?

Datafication, or in other words, the conversion of (human) behavior into data, has become an increasingly important topic in (mainstream) scientific research in recent years (e.g., Agostinho, 2019; Alemohammad, 2018; Bonde Thylstrup et al., 2019; Chen et al., 2012; Elish and Boyd, 2018; Flyverbom and Murray, 2018; Flyverbom et al., 2017; Hartmann and Henkel, 2020; Jones, 2019; Lycett, 2017; Newell and Marabelli, 2015). Although on the one hand it seems necessary for organizations to collect data in order to gain or maintain a competitive advantage (Casado and Bornstein, 2020; Günther et al., 2017), not everyone is positive about the value and ethical boundaries of collecting (big) data (e.g., Boyd and Crawford, 2012; Di Russo, 2020; Gitelman, 2013; Zuboff, 2019). Datafication is thus increasingly under review. However, although Big Data is a big topic, little is written in detail about what datafication actually means for organizations.

Especially, what data is about (the content) is often left out of consideration. This can have a fundamental influence on the development and ultimate consequences of AI systems (Faraj et al., 2018; Pachidi et al., 2021). The examples described in this chapter show that a suitable dataset does not appear out of nowhere. In order to ensure that AI systems fit in well with the intended work processes, a large part of the data should be organization- or domain-specific. This requires organizational and management activities to enable data construction, so as to ensure that sufficient data is available to train an AI system. The challenge is to enable and centralize data construction within the organization by, for example, adding it to the existing tasks of employees or even setting up new positions.

Additionally, a focus only on creating data is not enough. In order to arrive at a good, suitable dataset, it should be collected, 'cleaned up', and made suitable for use in the development of an AI system. Figure 5.1 provides a schematic overview of the actions that need to be taken regarding data preparation for machine learning (Jones, 2018). Datasets are thus not ready-made products; instead, they must be created. This takes a lot of time, energy and sometimes money (Savitz, 2012).

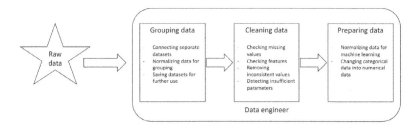

Figure 5.1   Steps for data preparation

When organizations decide to internally develop an AI system, an important challenge is whether the right data expertise is in-house. Creating datasets is a specialized skill. That is why more and more organizations decide to hire so-called data engineers, in addition to the data scientists who build the AI models. Data engineers are specifically involved in creating datasets that can be used to train AI systems (Willems, 2017). Questions such as 'What exactly do you need to do to achieve a good dataset?' are often difficult issues for organizations. By internally creating sufficient data and by also bringing the right expertise within an organization, both the quantity and quality of the data can be continuously maintained.

Another challenge in how to deal with datafication has to do with organizing responsibly for data. Of course, the right activities for data construction and ensuring the right data expertise lie at the heart of this, but this is not enough to be able to characterize it as responsible. Discussions about responsible data management often focus on privacy-related issues (e.g., Boyd and Crawford, 2012; Crawford and Schultz, 2014; Mai, 2016; Zuboff, 2019). In our cases we have seen that here, too, privacy – and finding a way to safeguard it – poses a challenge.

Organizing responsibly for data goes further, however, and also concerns, for example, awareness of what activities are undertaken with regard to datafication, and what influence these activities have on the final dataset and the algorithm (think, for example, of MultiCo, which has its employees perform online games). Furthermore, choices that are made regarding what data is (not) collected also have consequences for the AI system (for example, at Philadelphia the AI system is trained on data from a very specific group of clients; at CB only interaction content and not, for example, customer data is used).

Creating new data construction roles also poses challenges in responsibly organizing for data. For example, how do you ensure that (in the case of the LUMC) you guarantee the quality of the data when you have a group other than the domain experts who annotate the data? A final, important element of responsible organization for data has to do with the changing responsibilities that are becoming important. A central challenge is determining who will supervise, understand and ultimately be responsible for the construction of data.

5.3.2   Challenge 2: Should You Buy an Externally Developed System or Should You Develop It Internally?

A second challenge is whether you, as an organization, decide to purchase an externally developed AI system 'off the shelf', or whether you decide to develop an AI system internally (Krush, 2019; Pickup, 2019). The examples in section 5.2 have shown that, regardless of the choice for external versus internal, for a sufficient connection to the work processes it is necessary to have (part of) the data come from the organization itself. This presents challenges for both the external and the internal development (see Figure 5.2).

External development is attractive for organizations, because organizations such as data science startups that often develop these types of AI systems already have the necessary in-house expertise, and the organization that pur-

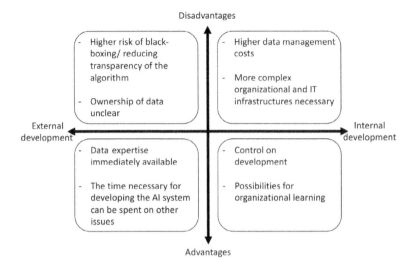

Figure 5.2   Advantages and disadvantages of external versus internal development

chases the AI system will not have to reinvent the wheel. Another advantage of external development is that the organization itself does not have to be directly involved in the development process. At the same time however, this creates the risk that it is no longer clear which data the AI system is being trained on, which reinforces the black-boxing of AI systems and makes them more difficult to use (Burrell, 2016; Faraj et al., 2018). When an organization chooses to develop the AI system externally, as MultiCo did, questions also arise about the ownership of the data once it has been transferred to the developer. Although external development thus seems to be an option, because it relieves the organization of this complicated and time-consuming process, external development does require close involvement of the organization in the first place in the development and use of the data.

A second option is to develop the system internally, as CB did. Organizations then keep the management of the system under their own control. Although this reduces or removes the problems surrounding a lack of insight and overview, it creates new challenges. For example, it means that for the internal development and training of the AI system, the data with which the system is trained should be stored in the organization. In many cases this means that data sources come together that were never previously available together in such a way. This makes the organization more vulnerable to larger-scale data leaks than if the data is stored in different silos. Also, not all organizations are prepared for what running AI systems requires of the internal servers, which often means they have insufficient capacity. The internal development of AI systems thus requires a renewed organizational and information technology infrastructure regarding (secure) organizing for data.

The choice between external or internal development of an AI system therefore does not have a one-size-fits-all solution. Both come with their own challenges. In addition, there is an overarching challenge, relating to both external and internal development: the better an organization wants to align the AI system with the work processes, the more the developer is dependent on correct and up-to-date data. This creates, by definition, a growing dependence between AI developers and organizations.

5.3.3 Challenge 3: How Do You Ensure that Data Specialists can Collaborate with Organizations?

In the two challenges described above, we emphasized the importance of developers and organizations working together in order to develop an effective AI system. However, this is not a process that can be expected to naturally go smoothly, as developers and organizations generally speak a very different language (Pachidi et al., 2021; Van den Broek et al., fothcoming; Zhang et al., 2020). Where organizations are focused on domain-specific knowledge and business operations, developers speak the computer language required for coding the machine learning algorithms (Slota et al., 2020).

It is therefore important for developers to have not only coding skills, but also social skills. These will ensure that developers understand more about the domain and are therefore better able to support the gathering of the right data. In addition, it is important for developers – for modelling and developing well-functioning algorithms – to be familiar with the domain they are developing for, for which they certainly need the social skills. When developers have a better understanding of practice, they can, to a certain extent,[2] filter out errors from the datasets and algorithms themselves. We will discuss this in more detail in Chapter 6.

Conversely, it is also necessary for organizations to take into account the possible need to educate users and employees regarding statistical knowledge. MultiCo showed, for example, to optimally involve HR professionals in data construction required new data-related knowledge. Examples of questions that users and employees should be able to answer when involved in organizing for data include: What could be white spots in data? Do we really want systems that are mainly based on past behaviour? Does the data used for the AI system avoid promoting too much homogeneity? How can certain choices regarding data construction affect profiling?

Organizing for data and developing AI systems is a continuous negotiation process between the developer and the user (Van den Broek et al., forthcoming; Zhang et al., 2020). To make this co-creation possible, more attention to the social skills for the developer and data and statistics training for the user are required. Only then can the users stay in the loop when it comes to AI systems.

5.4   SUMMARY

In this chapter, we have discussed one of the most important building blocks of AI: data. We have shown that datasets do not simply exist, but should be carefully composed. This is a complex and laborious process with consequences for work and for the resulting AI system. Managing AI in practice therefore first requires organizing for data. We concluded the chapter by describing some of the challenges of organizing for data. Of course, simply organizing for data is not enough for the successful development and implementation of AI in practice. Once a first version of the AI system has been developed, the next step is to test and validate it. We will discuss this further in the next chapter.

BOX 5.1   KEY TAKEAWAYS

- Organizing for data involves new data-related tasks. These can be performed by existing employees, or new positions can be created.
- To develop an AI system that aligns with the intended work processes, developers should sufficiently understand the context-related data.
- Data-related tasks directly affect the AI system. It is therefore important to educate employees about data and statistics.
- Because of the influence of data-related tasks, it is important to handle those tasks with care, approach these ethically, and to take into account the possible consequences of choices from the outset.

NOTES

1. The developer's name remains anonymous for privacy reasons.
2. Due to the self-learning nature of AI systems, it is no longer always possible for data scientists to understand where certain errors were made during the development of the system.

REFERENCES

Agostinho, D. (2019). The optical unconscious of Big Data: Datafication of vision and care for unknown futures. *Big Data and Society*, *6*(1), 1–10.

Alemohammad, H. (2018). Creating a machine learning commons for global development. https://medium.com/radiant-earth-insights/creating-a-machine-learning -commons-for-global-development-256ef3dd46aa

Bonde Thylstrup, N., Flyverbom, M., & Helles, R. (2019). Datafied knowledge production: Introduction to the special theme. *Big Data and Society*, *6*(2), 1–5.

Boyd, D., & Crawford, K. (2012). Critical questions for big data: Provocations for a cultural, technological, and scholarly phenomenon. *Information, Communication and Society*, *15*(5), 662–679.

Burrell, J. (2016). How the machine 'thinks': Understanding opacity in machine learning algorithms. *Big Data and Society*, *3*(1), 1–12.

Casado, M., & Bornstein, M. (2020). The new business of AI (and how it's different from traditional software). https://a16z.com/2020/02/16/the-new-business-of-ai-and -how-its-different-from-traditional-software/.

Chen, H., Chiang, R.H.L., & Storey, V.C. (2012). Business intelligence and analytics: From big data to big impact. *MIS Quarterly*, *35*(4), 1165–1188.

Crawford, K., & Schultz, J. (2014). Big data and due process: Toward a framework to redress predictive privacy harms. *Boston College Law Review*, *55*(1), 93–128.

Davenport, T.H., Barth, P., & Bean, R. (2012). How 'big data' is different. *MIT Sloan Management Review*, *54*(1), 22–24.

Di Russo, J. (2020). Bye bye Big Data! https://towardsdatascience.com/bye-bye-big -data-fbea187c7739.

Elish, M.C., & Boyd, D. (2018). Situating methods in the magic of Big Data and AI. *Communication Monographs*, *85*(1), 57–80.

Faraj, S., Pachidi, S., & Sayegh, K. (2018). Working and organizing in the age of the learning algorithm. *Information and Organization*, *28*(1), 62–70.

Flyverbom, M., Madsen, A.K., & Rasche, A. (2017). Big Data as governmentality in international development: Digital traces, algorithms, and altered visibilities. *Information Society*, *33*, 35–42.

Flyverbom, M., & Murray, J. (2018). Datastructuring – Organizing and curating digital traces into action. *Big Data and Society*, *5*(2), 1–12.

Gitelman, L. (2013). *Raw data is an oxymoron.* Cambridge, MA: MIT press.

Günther, W.A., Mehrizi, M.H.R., Huysman, M.H., & Feldberg, F. (2017). Debating big data: A literature review on realizing value from big data. *Journal of Strategic Information Systems*, *26*(3), 191–209.

Hartmann, P., & Henkel, J. (2020). The rise of corporate science in AI: Data as a strategic resource. *Academy of Management Discoveries*, *6*(3), 359–381.

Jones, M. (2019). What we talk about when we talk about (big) data. *Journal of Strategic Information Systems*, *28*(1), 3–16.

Jones, T.M. (2018). Data, structure, and the data science pipeline. https://developer.ibm .com/articles/ba-intro-data-science-1/.

Krush, A. (2019). Off-the-shelf AI: Adopting much-hyped technology with minimum risk. https://www.objectstyle.com/machine-learning/off-the-shelf-ai-and-machine -learning.

Lycett, M. (2017). 'Datafication': Making sense of (big) data in a complex world. *European Journal of Information Systems*, *22*(4), 381–386.

Mai, J.E. (2016). Big data privacy: The datafication of personal information. *Information Society*, *32*(3), 192–199.

McAfee, A., Brynjolfsson, E., Davenport, T.H., Patil, D.J., & Barton, D. (2012). Big data: The management revolution. *Harvard Business Review*, *90*(10), 60–68.

Newell, S., & Marabelli, M. (2015). Strategic opportunities (and challenges) of algorithmic decision-making: A call for action on the long-term societal effects of 'datification'. *Journal of Strategic Information Systems*, *24*(1), 3–14.

O'Neil, C. (2016). *Weapons of math destruction: How big data increases inequality and threatens democracy*. New York: Crown.

Pachidi, S., Berends, H., Faraj, S., & Huysman, M. (2021). Make way for the algorithms: Symbolic actions and change in a regime of knowing. *Organization Science*, *32*(1), 18–41.

Pickup, O. (2019). Are off-the-shelf AI tools a good idea? https://www.raconteur.net/technology/ai-tools-pre-built.

Savitz, E. (2012) The big cost of Big Data. https://www.forbes.com/sites/ciocentral/2012/04/16/the-big-cost-of-big-data/#5ae1742c5a3b.

Slota, S.C., Hoffman, A.S., Ribes, D., & Bowker, G.C. (2020). Prospecting (in) the data sciences. *Big Data and Society*, *7*(1), 1–12.

Van den Broek, E., Sergeeva, A., & Huysman, M.H. (forthcoming) When the machine meets the expert: An ethnography of developing AI for hiring. *MIS Quarterly*.

Von Krogh, G. (2018). Artificial intelligence in organizations: New opportunities for phenomenon-based theorizing. *Academy of Management Discoveries*, *4*(4), 404–409.

Willems, K. (2017). Data scientist vs. data engineer. https://www.datacamp.com/community/blog/data-scientist-vs-data-engineer?utm_source=adwords_ppc&utm_campaignid=9942305733&utm_adgroupid=100189364546&utm_device=c&utm_keyword=&utm_matchtype=b&utm_network=g&utm_adpostion=&utm_creative=229765585183&utm_targetid=aud-392016246653:dsa-929501846124&utm_loc_interest_ms=&utm_loc_physical_ms=1010543&gclid=CjwKCAjw26H3BRB2EiwAy32zhdORerOrc65XFrlqnmZIR5bQg9WDB3w41e7278skP2z5khN6lFIvXRoC-rcQAvD_BwE.

Zhang, Z., Nandhakumar, J., Hummel, J., & Waardenburg, L. (2020). Addressing the key challenges of developing machine learning AI systems for knowledge-intensive work. *MIS Quarterly Executive*, *19*(4), 221–238.

Zuboff, S. (2019). *The age of surveillance capitalism: The fight for a human future at the new frontier of power*. London: Profile Books.

6. Testing and validating

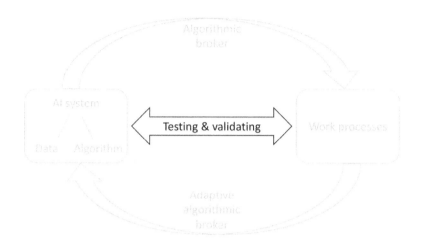

Figure 6.0   *Overview of core themes: Chapter 6*

6.1   INTRODUCTION

In this chapter, we discuss a second important aspect that requires specific attention in the implementation of an artificial intelligence (AI) system: testing and validating. Issues in computer science are often about whether and how an AI system works (e.g., Hosny et al., 2018; Salganik et al., 2020). These frequently concern questions regarding the measurability of outcomes and which methods lead to the best results (testing), and whether these outcomes are of added value (validation). Using the cases in this book, we want to look at this from a management perspective, for the question of when an AI system is good enough to implement is not only a technical issue (Burton et al., 2020), but also a management issue.

Little is known about how management decides whether an AI system is performing sufficiently in order to be implemented by an organization. As a result, it may appear that testing and validating AI is the sole responsibility of data scientists. Yet, when implementing AI systems in an organization, management makes the ultimate choice of whether or not to do so. This lack of understanding of the considerations of management in the implementation of AI calls for more insight into how organizations handle the testing and validation of AI systems.

As AI systems can automate more and more tasks which previously were undertaken by humans, they can have major consequences for people and society as a whole. After all, AI systems can potentially decide whether or not you will be hired, can generate diagnoses, or partly take over the care of a patient. The question of whether a system is 'good enough' to take over such processes from humans is therefore of great importance. Yet, the question remains: How do you determine whether a system is 'good enough' to be put into use? Due to the complexity of AI systems, the way in which outcomes are generated are difficult to explain; that is, black-boxed (see also Chapter 2). If you do not know how the results come about, who can then be held responsible for determining whether they are 'good enough'?

Our cases indicate that technical requirements and guidelines that AI systems must comply with are often in place. These conditions can be set by the organization, but also, for example, by the user. We give an example of both options. However, testing and validating AI in organizations does not end with meeting such 'hard' conditions. The cases show that including work processes is also an essential part of the testing and validation process. In addition, management should take into account the trust and expectations of users with regard to the AI system. Guidelines play a role here, but it is also important to involve and train users and developers. Based on the cases, we discuss best practices for responsible testing and validation of AI and conclude this chapter with a look at the challenges.

6.2   TESTING AND VALIDATING IN PRACTICE

In this section, the cases of ABN AMRO, KLM and Volkswagen highlight what it means for organizations if AI has to meet strict conditions, what these conditions could entail, and how an organization can comply with them. The police and Philadelphia show how the surrounding work processes can also have a major influence on the testing and validation of AI. For the question of how this can take place in a responsible manner, we return to the cases of KLM and Philadelphia.

6.2.1   Validating using Technical Conditions and Guidelines

Testing and validating AI in organizations often means that it should meet certain technical conditions that have been set within or outside the organization. At KLM, clear technical conditions are set by the users. In addition, users have also set requirements for the preconditions of implementation. ABN AMRO operates in a highly regulated context, meaning that there are many internal and external guidelines that an AI system must comply with. This example shows that compliance with set requirements does not merely concern technical standards; internal and external regulatory guidelines should also be included, which can also influence the technical capabilities of the AI system. Volkswagen is an example of a system that is assessed on the basis of its technical capabilities, independent of the work context, and demonstrates what happens if you only take these 'hard' conditions into account when testing and validating.

KLM: consumption prediction
KLM developed its own the Meals-on-Board System (MOBS) to better match catering to the specific demand for meals during the flight. Before the development of this AI system, KLM Catering Services (KCS, the user of MOBS) used a simple linear system (not based on AI) to make catering calculations. This old system was offered by a third party, for which KLM paid €400 000 per year. These costs, and the possibilities of using AI to create a more dynamic system, have been the triggers for KLM to find out whether it could develop a more advanced – and at the same time cheaper – system itself.

From the moment KLM decided to develop a system internally, the developers had four months to demonstrate that they could create a well-functioning system. During this process, KLM's priority was: 'operation always continues'. So, if the AI system brought even the smallest possible uncertainty, this gave KCS reason to opt out and stay with the expensive existing tool. In addition, KCS set a number of technical conditions the system should meet during testing and validation:

1. The coverage ratio of the number of flights for which predictions are made with the MOBS should in any case be equal to the number of flights for which calculations are made with the old system.
2. The prediction percentage should be higher than what the users would normally arrive at using the old system.
3. The mean absolute error and the standard deviation error (the deviations between the predicted number of passengers and the actual number of passengers) should be at least equal to the deviation that the users normally have when using the old system.

In short, the user's overall requirement was that the MOBS provided more accurate and more stable predictions than the existing system. In order to convince the employees of the catering services of the added value and accuracy of the MOBS, KLM decided during testing and validation to run the new system parallel to the existing work processes. In this way the users could see for themselves that predictions of the MOBS were indeed better than what they had been able to achieve with the old system.

What is also interesting in the case of KLM is that the users set technical requirements not only for the system, but also for how the team of developers is organized. For example, it required 24/7 IT support for the implementation of this technologically complex system. In order to be able to provide the service, the IT service rosters had to be restructured to also include night shifts. Managing the testing and validation of the AI system at KLM therefore related not only to the system itself, but also to the work processes of the IT service. In section 6.2.2 we will further address such changes in work processes.

ABN AMRO: money laundering prediction
Between the end of 2019 and the beginning of 2020, ABN AMRO's data scientists trained the algorithm they use for the supervised model of the AML system. This was done in a so-called 'sandbox' test environment: a shielded space in which a system can be tested, without other programs present that could possibly disrupt its operation. Among other things, the data scientists were engaged in validating their models from a data science perspective by, among other things, checking the assumptions and training the models to generate an effective performance for the developers.

However, the data scientists' testing and validation activities were not sufficient for the organization to proceed to implementation. Due to the highly regulated institutional context in which ABN AMRO operates, testing and validation also implies obtaining a large number of approvals for the AI system at different levels of legislation and regulation and for different (sub) purposes. Specifically, they must obtain approval in four different areas.

First, the risks of the change from the current to the new situation needed to be identified and assessed by means of a change risk assessment. An overview was made of these risks, after which the chance that something goes wrong and the possible consequences, should this happen, were examined for each risk. The combination of impact and probability determines the risk factor. The change risk assessment also looks at any mitigating measures and their effect on the impact and likelihood of risks.

Second, a so-called data protection impact assessment needed to be completed. This is a risk analysis with regard to the data used in the system. This assessment examines, for example, what the possible risks of developing and using an AI system will be for the bank's customers and for society. This assessment tests for biases (for example, whether the model leads to bias on customer groups or type of transactions) and looks at how the impact and likelihood of these risks can be mitigated.

Third, the models were internally validated by an independent department specialized in this area. Separately from the data scientists, they carried out an extensive assessment of the model, mainly looking at its quality and the extent to which it is suitable for the intended purpose.

Fourth, the Risk Committee considered the risks that may accompany the transition to a new model. Here, it was important that well-considered choices were made with regard to the use of the models and that they fitted within the bank's so-called 'risk appetite'.

Volkswagen: smart powerplants
In the DataLab, the data scientists at Volkswagen have the opportunity to develop applications based on their own academic and/or social interests (see also Chapter 4). One of these applications is the 'smart powerplant': an AI system for continuously determining the optimal adjustment of generators in factories, enabling full automation of the generator's settings. The freedom given to the data scientists to develop AI systems also means that testing and validation of the system is focused on whether the system works in terms of data science, thus in technical ways; whether the developer has made the right choices in building and training the model. In the case of the smart powerplant AI system, the tests indicated that the model can reduce a powerplant's emissions by 20 per cent, which was reason enough for the developers to consider the system to be (technically) 'valid'.

After testing the smart powerplant AI system to their standards, the data scientists offered the system to the power plant managers responsible for its implementation. Since the work processes had not been included in the testing and validation, no guidelines had been drawn up for the implementation and use of the smart powerplants. As it turns out, the power plant managers were far from eager to outsource this part of their work, and had plenty of room to let the system affect their work as little as possible.

The use of the system in practice is only minimal: the power plant managers agreed to receive a daily e-mail containing a suggestion for the generator's settings generated by the AI system. In this way, the power plant managers remain in control over the setup. In addition, the data scientists have no insight into whether suggestions of the AI system are actually being implemented and whether the technically reasoned 20 per cent reduction in emissions is indeed achieved by means of the AI system. Consequently, there is no validation.

Volkswagen demonstrates how strict requirements can be imposed on the technical functioning of a system, but that this does not necessarily have a positive influence on the actual use of the system. KLM and ABN AMRO go further, and show two different ways in which requirements for testing and validating AI systems can be set that go beyond making accurate predictions. In the case of ABN AMRO, the requirements come from both within the organization and the external environment. In view of the bank's strictly regulated context, new systems must meet certain technical and regulatory conditions. In the case of KLM, the technical requirements are mainly determined by the user. It wants a system that certainly works better than how it has set up its work processes up to that point, both in the accuracy of the calculations and in the stability of the system. In addition, KLM's requirements are not only aimed at the system itself, but also at the work processes around it.

6.2.2   Work Processes as Part of Validation

It is important to consider that not only the technical functioning of the AI system is necessary, but also embedding it in the existing work processes it is intended to support. In the example of the police, the developers indicate which organizational and work adjustments are necessary. In the case of Philadelphia, it is the organization that indicates how the system can properly support the work process.

Police: predictive policing
The police developed CAS to predict where and when chances of crime are highest. In order to test and validate CAS in practice, the project team carried out a pilot in four different cities in the Netherlands. To this end, they wrote a pilot plan for the police authorities. The plan described, for example, the intended goals of the pilot and the success criteria for both the use and the effects of the AI system. The CAS pilot plan as written by the project team contained two technical requirements:

1. During the pilot phase, an area should score better on the number of registered, related offences than a control area where CAS is not applied. Scoring better means: (a) a greater decrease in registered, related crime within a certain period than in a control area; or (b) a less sharp increase in related offences than in a control area.
2. During the pilot phase, an area should score better on the total number of registered crimes than a control area where CAS is not applied. Scoring better can mean: (a) a greater decrease in registered crime within a certain period than in a control area; or (b) a less sharp increase in registered crime than in a control area.

In addition to the technical details, the project team also mentioned another, more notable list of aspects that determine whether the AI system is considered successful. This has nothing to do with the technical capabilities and results of the CAS, but with the work processes of the users. According to the pilot plan, the participating police departments should:

- work with CAS;
- be able to independently generate CAS results in the internal police system;
- be able to draw up deployment advice for police activities based on the CAS results;
- create work orders for the officers that are applicable to the predictions of CAS;
- manage patrols via operational managers;
- ensure that police officers know of CAS; and
- ensure that police officers conduct patrols in accordance with CAS results.

In the last three months of 2015, the pilot was carried out at four different police stations across the Netherlands.[1] The testing and validation was carried out by employees of the Police Academy, who later wrote an evaluation on this (Mali et al., 2017). The evaluation showed that the intended results were achieved at three of the four stations. Based on this 75 per cent score, the evaluators decided to call the pilot a success, and the CAS was gradually implemented nationally in the years that followed.

In the evaluation report, however, the work processes regarding the use of CAS were also critically examined, and it was concluded that steps should be taken to reorganize this, which also required guidelines on how the results of the AI system have to be used. As a result, new responsibilities were formed, which we discuss in more detail in Chapter 7.

Philadelphia: social robotics
Due to the limited knowledge about the influence of social robots in health-care, Philadelphia regularly tests and validates the social robot application during a multi-year, controlled experiment. Philadelphia has set two central goals (or criteria for success), which focus on the client and are carefully considered at every step of the development:

1. The robot supports the client in increasing self-reliance/independence.
2. The robot helps to improve the client's quality of life.

For Philadelphia, testing and validating the social robot does not depend on a short-term pilot, as is the case in previous examples. Instead, they see each robot stay in the experiment as a pilot, where the robot is carefully tested, validated and adjusted according to the development goals.

If a new step in the development of the system does not benefit these goals, to Philadelphia this is not a reason to immediately discontinue. Instead, taking into account how the goals are affected is an opportunity for reflection and gives reason to go back to the drawing board and continue with 'plan B'. On the other hand, if a step in the development contributes to these goals, this offers extra motivation to continue.

For the process of testing and validation, Philadelphia set up interdisciplinary robot teams, which consist of healthcare professionals and AI developers. During the first development of the social robot Phi, the team meetings were mainly about defining a shared vision for the development of the technology with questions such as: What should the robot be technically capable of? Then, in the phase of testing and validation it is not so much about refining the technical aspects any more, it is about further adapting Phi so that it can contribute to the two criteria for success. With this in mind, each robot stay is evaluated with the entire robot team, which is necessary to better understand how the technical possibilities can come together with the more social criteria to validate the robot.

The above examples demonstrate how important it is to involve the work processes that already exist when testing and validating AI. We have seen that this can be done in several ways. With the police, the developers themselves set the conditions for the work process, and after testing, advice was issued to the project team by a group of independent evaluators. At Philadelphia, the organization sets conditions for what is important in the work process and the robot team adjusts its testing and validation strategy accordingly. Involving the work process in the testing and validation of an AI system means that users should be actively involved.

6.2.3   Managing Expectations and Trust

If not only the technical aspects of an AI system have to be tested and validated, but the work processes also have to be taken into account, there is a considerable chance that the users have to be more involved in this process. However, knowledge about data science is often not present among users, which can result in incorrect or too-high expectations, or a lack of confidence in the AI system. KLM and Philadelphia highlight how organizations, by undertaking activities to educate users with regard to data science knowledge, are able to manage expectations and confidence in the hard-to-fathom AI systems.

KLM: consumption prediction
The KLM development team worked hard to get its MOBS to a level where it met the technical requirements set in terms of performance (see section 6.2.1). However, the technical requirements were not the only criteria for testing and validating the system. Especially in organizations such as KLM where operations must always continue, it is very important that technology connects

seamlessly with the work processes. KLM therefore involved the users of the catering services department in the first phase of testing the AI system.

Automating how many meals should be loaded on board requires users to have enough confidence in MOBS to leave the decision to the AI system. Due to the complexity and difficulty of explaining the system, developing trust with users cannot be taken for granted. In addition, as is often the case with the implementation of AI systems (see Chapter 3), users fear that their work will be taken over. According to the project manager, it is important that users start to see the system as a 'gift' rather than a 'threat'.

To foster trust, the development team states that it is important for developers and users to better understand each other. In order to allow the developers to better understand what the 'dynamic work' actually entails, the team organized a day at the Schiphol Pier, where all operational processes are carried out. Conversely, it is also important to transfer knowledge to the user about the technical possibilities of AI systems, including the methods. In order to manage trust and expectations of the users, the development team decided to provide an AI mini-course for the users. This course started with an explanation of how a basic decision tree works and concluded with a more advanced explanation of machine learning techniques. In this course, the developers also showed what outcomes this system could (not) generate and how these should be interpreted. In this way, they aimed to manage the expectations regarding the capabilities of the AI system.

However, offering such a mini-course is not a self-evident activity. For the developers, it was a fun and often new experience, but at the same time also a tiring process, because the transfer of knowledge certainly does not happen automatically. Initially, for the developers it felt like a battle between 'camp ratio' (developers) and 'camp expertise' (users). Nonetheless, the upskilling of users ensured that work processes could be actively involved in testing and validating AI systems. Moreover, this process offered valuable work-related insights that could be used in the development process.

Philadelphia: social robotics
The testing and validation of the social robot Phi comprises a multi-year programme. Due to the experimental nature of this phase, it is important that clients interact with the robot in a natural way as much as possible during the first robot stays. The spontaneous interaction between client and robot gives the robot team 'natural' interaction data which they can then use to 'feed' the robot. In addition, managing the expectations clients have regarding the robot from an ethical perspective is important. Too-high expectations can, for example, lead to uncertainty or disappointment, negatively affecting the client's quality of life, which of course is the opposite of Philadelphia's intentions and a core part of its validation criteria (see section 6.2.2).

With the first robot stay, clients receive a so-called communication book. This book lists the basic rules for using the robot. In addition, during the first stay, most of the attention is devoted to further educating the clients regarding the (in)capabilities of the robot. In this way, the team tries to manage the expectations of clients. Philadelphia is especially sensitive to the fact that the ideas and expectations a client may have of a social robot may be misleading. For instance, clients may expect it to act like any other 'normal' person. Vulnerable people may not be able to understand the limits of these technologies or determine what such a robot is when compared to a human. Managing the client's expectations in advance is thus of central importance to Philadelphia.

The above examples provide two reasons why it is important to manage the expectations and trust of the users for the testing and validation of AI systems in practice. At KLM, it was mainly about ensuring that the operational processes were not hindered during the testing of an AI system, and that they remained of at least the same quality when the system was implemented. At Philadelphia, it is about finding a balance between the training and knowledge transfer necessary in order to, on the one hand, get the most out of the tests so that the robot can be improved, while on the other hand, guaranteeing the well-being of the client.

6.3   THE CHALLENGES OF TESTING AND VALIDATING

Expectations of AI are high (Brynjolfsson and McAfee, 2014). At the same time, a fear exists that AI does not have a moral compass, allowing it to make unethical decisions or unnecessarily sideline people. This causes many organizations to experience pressure to do 'something' with AI, which feeds the fear of missing the boat and thus lagging too far behind in the AI-embracing competition. The high expectations are characteristic of all new technologies and increase the risk that its implementation is done too quickly, often resulting in discontinuing its operation. However, where it used to be that not thoroughly validated technologies resulted in obsolescence and financial loss, in the case of AI the consequences can be more comprehensive. Consider, for example, the widespread media attention to Amazon's recruitment algorithm that had to be disabled due to the disadvantagement of female candidates. A thorough testing and validation process is therefore essential to prevent organizations from following the AI hype all too easily.

The question of when a technology is good enough for implementation is an extra challenging question when it comes to AI systems. Since AI can take over tasks that were previously under human control, the system can have potentially major consequences for people, organizations and society. The question of who is responsible for these decisions is therefore of great importance, but difficult to answer, for the complexity and self-learning properties of these systems ensure that it is difficult or impossible to explain how certain decisions came about. In section 6.2 we have described the various factors that should be included in the testing and validation process. These are summarized in Figure 6.1.

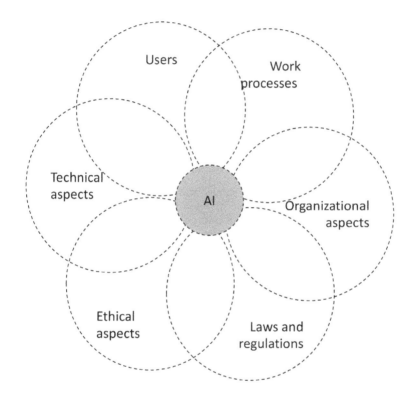

Figure 6.1   Factors involved in testing and validating AI systems

In this section we will further examine the question: How can these factors be included in the testing and validation process, and what are the roles and responsibilities of different actors in this process? Specifically, we will discuss the following three challenges:

1. What is the role of developers in the testing and validation process?
2. How do you take into account internal and external laws, regulations and guidelines during testing and validation?

3. How do you involve the users and work processes when testing and
    validating?

6.3.1   Challenge 1: What is the Role of Developers in the Testing and Validation Process?

As described in Chapter 5, data and the resulting algorithms are not objective
and independent, but the result of choices made by people. Algorithms are
infused with the (un)conscious choices made by their designers. The choices
in data (for example, what is or is not measured), the type of algorithm and
the weight given to factors reflect the values, beliefs and ethical standards of
developers (O'Neil, 2016). These decisions are not necessarily the result of
a collective decision or discussed in a code of conduct, but are often made
informally and intuitively by an individual designer (Faraj et al., 2018).
Norms, prejudices, existing work characteristics and personal character traits
inevitably influence, often largely invisibly, how an AI system works (Ananny
and Crawford, 2018). The development of an AI system is thus a sociotechnical process, involving continuous interaction between technology and humans.

Developers therefore play a crucial role in designing a valid and ethically
responsible AI system. To do this properly, developers will have to look beyond
the technical issues (for example: How do I optimally model the patterns in my
data?) and conditions (for example, predictions should be accurate in at least
90 per cent of the cases). Consider, for example, the case of CB compared
to Philadelphia. While a natural language processing algorithm in a chatbot,
aimed at handling customer questions, can occasionally afford a mistake in its
choice of words, this is out of the question for Phi, due to the vulnerable people
with whom the care robot interacts. While the techniques may be similar for
the developers in both cases, the testing and validation process is very different. What is more, a neural network that is highly advanced may seem like the
best option in theory (from the perspective of computer science), but in the
context of the organization this is not the case at all due to, for example, a lack
of server capacity. Thus, involving the organizational context in testing and
validating an AI system is crucial for developers.

The choices in the development of an AI system thus play a central role
in generating the AI outcomes, which can have both technical and ethical
consequences. That is why, in discussions about the social acceptability of
AI systems, the explainability of a system is now often seen as an essential
condition. General Data Protection Regulation (GDPR) legislation in Europe
has even included this as an explicit condition, and many ethical guidelines
also point to the importance of explainability.[2] While this may sound nice,
explaining how a complex AI system makes certain decisions is nearly impos-

sible, also for those who designed the system (Faraj et al., 2018; O'Neil, 2016). Additionally, the consequences of AI systems do not only depend on the technical explainability, but are also related to the context of use. Therefore, the challenge for management is to go beyond the technical explainability. Box 6.1 provides a number of examples of questions that managers could ask to arrive at a broader explanation.

BOX 6.1 EXAMPLES OF MANAGEMENT QUESTIONS

Data

- Which (parts of) datasets were used and why?
- Has the data been checked for certain under- or over-represented groups?
- Is the data representative of the relevant work processes?

Algorithm

- How was the existing problem translated into a model?
- What can the model do (and what not)?
- Have the results been checked for hidden prejudices? If so, has the model been adapted/corrected, and how?

Organization

- Do we have the right in-house experts to be able to check the algorithm in the work context and to understand its implications?
- How do the results relate to the current way of working?
- What are the consequences for the targeted and supporting work processes?

In response to the need to make AI systems technically explainable and to ensure responsible development of AI, the importance of an independent, external auditor of AI systems is increasingly being emphasized (e.g., Guszca et al., 2018). Monitoring AI systems is a role that we increasingly see consultants taking on. The risk of this is that they do not know enough about the work process to assess the possible consequences of the system, while our examples indicate that it is precisely the validation based on the detailed work processes that is essential to develop a valuable system.

6.3.2   Challenge 2: How Do You Take into Account Internal and External Laws, Regulations and Guidelines During Testing and Validation?

When the decision to develop an AI system is made, it is important to map out the legal framework within which the system will be developed and used. As the ABN AMRO case demonstrates, it is very important to include this in a targeted manner throughout the development process. In general, there are three levels that are important in mapping these guidelines and regulations.

First of all, what is the legal and regulatory context, including rules and regulations that should be taken into account in the design and development process? In addition to legislation for the specific context, data legislation such as the GDPR are of course important for almost every organization. Such legislation also partly determines the freedom of movement that organizations have when using AI. For example, Article 22 of the GDPR states that, as a human being: 'The data subject shall have the right not to be subject to a decision based solely on automated processing, including profiling, which produces legal effects concerning him or her or similarly significantly affects him or her'.

In other words: you are entitled to a human perspective or opinion in the case of automatically made decisions that can have a major impact on you. Thus, regardless of how much an organization invests in developing AI systems capable of taking over certain tasks, its scope is also determined by the legislative authorities.

In addition, legislation does not always keep pace with technical developments; amendments to the law are slow, because government agencies often do not have a direct insight into what is needed within organizations. There may even be contradictory laws and regulations, which means that as an organization you have to make your own decisions or may even be faced with an impossible choice. For example, some organizations are expected to commit to detecting or combating fraud, but the data they want to use for this is protected under the GDPR. Which rules take precedence?

Due to the boundaries that legislation and regulations (rightly) impose on organizations, it is important to be aware of the legal and ethical frameworks very early on in the testing and validation process. It may also be advisable to cooperate with legislative authorities in order to arrive at appropriate legislation and regulations more quickly.

Secondly, in the testing and validation process, the institutional context should be mapped out. In the case of Philadelphia (and also the LUMC), for example, there are important healthcare guidelines at play. Organizations with a public function, such as banks, the police force or the judiciary, are under a social magnifying glass and can make less mistakes than, for example, a logistics company that uses AI to create smarter schedules. The consequences of such a magnifying glass are clearly visible in the criticism surrounding the American predictive policing AI system PredPol. This system takes little account of the danger of profiling when data on individuals is included. This has led to a great deal of social criticism, because a government body should actually prevent profiling. As a result of the ongoing criticism, several states have now discontinued the use of PredPol.

For management, it is important to analyse at an early stage what influence the institutional context has on the implementation of AI systems, and how much risk the organization can and is willing to take. In our preliminary research for selecting the cases, we noticed that many organizations are reluctant to provide openness. We noticed the fear of getting bad press, which mainly involved inciting resistance and damage to their image. This does not seem to be without reason; we have spoken to several organizations that had bad experiences with disclosure because, for example, a journalist gave a distorted image of reality in their opinion, which could also endanger the progress of projects internally. We certainly do not want to discourage organizations from using the possibilities AI offers, but we do point out that careful considerations should be made.

Thirdly, the guidelines from the internal organization should be included in drafting the testing and validation criteria. This may include internal regulations, as well as the necessary approvals and internal support required for the system to function properly. To prepare this analysis, one can ask questions such as: What risks are we willing to take and who determines this; for example, the chance that an incorrect assessment is made? What are the minimum quality requirements set for the organization; what must the system comply to, for example, what minimum customer satisfaction score should a chatbot achieve; and to what extent does the system contribute to the diversity goals of the organization? Answering questions about external and internal laws and regulations and guidelines helps to ensure that the AI system meets the requirements set. However, this does not guarantee that the AI system can be incorporated into the work processes without any problems. This also requires the user to be involved in the testing and validation process.

6.3.3 Challenge 3: How Do You Involve the Users and Work Processes when Testing and Validating?

As we have seen in our cases, it may be that, in practice, technically well-functioning systems turn out to have no value at all. Think of Volkswagen, for example, where a technically functioning and explainable system is still not sufficient to achieve optimal usage. In order to make an AI system not only technical, but also socially effective, there is an important challenge in terms of promoting and articulating the voice of employees during the design and implementation of AI. One way to ensure this is to involve users in the development process at an early stage. People who have a good understanding of the work processes are extremely valuable for achieving effective collaboration between users and developers. They understand the context of the data on which the system is trained and can, for example, help to check that there are no distortions in the results of the model.

Additionally, the expertise of users is essential for drawing up and assessing the validation criteria (Raisch and Krakowski, 2021). In order to allow users and experts to condider relevant validation criteria, further training in coding and computational skills is required. Writing and reading codes and designing algorithms is a specialized skill and requires knowledge that is not directly accessible to most people. Programming language differs from human language; for example, codes are strictly adhered to logical rules and require completeness and precision in order to be read. Insights into which data is used as input and how the system is trained are therefore important to understand the (im)possibilities of these systems and to create trust and the right expectations (Burrell, 2016; Glikson and Wooley, 2020).

When involving the user in the testing and validation process, feelings of resistance or fear of the AI system may pose a challenge. Mistrust may focus on the question of whether the system is even capable of taking over parts of the work, and the black-boxed nature of AI systems makes building trust even more difficult. In order to prepare users and management for the use of AI, it is again important to involve the user in the development process. Just as important in testing and validation is to investigate how the decisions taken relate to how users themselves would come to decisions. A possible strategy to gain user confidence in the system is to temporarily run the AI system in parallel with the old way of working, as was done at KLM and ABN AMRO. Critically comparing the results with the current way of working is also a valuable contribution that users can make to the testing and validation process.

Another source of resistance can come from fear of the consequences for one's own job. Uncertainty regarding the intentions behind the system feeds this fear. It is therefore important – through dialogue – to articulate clearly what the intended objectives are for the introduction of the AI system and what the expected contribution is of this technology to the work process. Which parts of the work will be automated and which new tasks will be added? Should I view the AI system as a colleague who supports me in my work, relieves me by taking over certain routine tasks, or more as a 'colleague expert' who offers advice? Many of these points are difficult to assess in advance; these changes should also be monitored over time and discussed regularly with the parties involved. We will address this in more detail in Chapter 8.

Finally, we would like to emphasize that testing and validating in and with work processes is not something that takes place by means of a series of interviews, by spending a day in the workplace or by conducting a survey. In order for the system to connect well with and contribute to work, continuous coordination and interaction between developers, management and domain experts is necessary. This is essential from the very beginning until well after the implementation phase.

6.4   SUMMARY

In this chapter, we have discussed that the question of when an AI system is good enough to proceed to implementation is not only technical, but also managerial. On the basis of our cases, we discussed that an AI system, logically, should function well technically and comply with the applicable laws and regulations; and to also be able to take ethical responsibility, there are ethical guidelines that can (or actually should) be taken into account. We have also shown that in order to achieve a well-functioning AI system, it is just as important to test and validate the system in relation to the work processes, the user and the organizational conditions. We discussed that testing and validating, especially with AI, requires extra attention because the possible consequences of underperforming systems for work and organizations can be major. Since the way in which such technology comes to conclusions is difficult to explain, the question 'Who is responsible for the final decisions?' is extra complicated.

BOX 6.2   KEY TAKEAWAYS

- A technically well-functioning system does not necessarily provide added value in practice, for this also requires a socially well-functioning system.
- Managing the testing and validation process requires constant coordination between a team of developers, users and management. Testing and validating an AI system requires knowledge of the technical properties of the system, laws and regulations, ethical guidelines, the context of the organization, the work processes and the user. Validating AI requires involving the user, to alleviate fear and mistrust.

NOTES

1.   Hoorn, Enschede, The Hague and Groningen.

2.   High Level Expert Group on AI Ethics Guidelines for Trustworthy AI (2019).

REFERENCES

Ananny, M., & Crawford, K. (2018). Seeing without knowing: Limitations of the transparency ideal and its application to algorithmic accountability. *New Media and Society*, 20(3), 973–989.

Brynjolfsson, E., & McAfee, A. (2014). *The second machine age: Work, progress, and prosperity in a time of brilliant technologies.* New York: W.W. Norton & Company.

Burrell, J. (2016). How the machine 'thinks': Understanding opacity in machine learning algorithms. *Big Data and Society*, 3(1). doi:10.1177/2053951715622512.

Burton, S., Habli, I., Lawton, T., McDermid, J., Morgan, P., & Porter, Z. (2020). Mind the gaps: Assuring the safety of autonomous systems from an engineering, ethical, and legal perspective. *Artificial Intelligence*, *279.* DOI: 10.1016/j.artint.2019.103201.

Faraj, S., Pachidi, S., & Sayegh, K. (2018). Working and organizing in the age of the learning algorithm. *Information and Organization*, 28(1), 62–70.

Glikson, E., & Woolley, A.W. (2020). Human trust in artificial intelligence: Review of empirical research. *Academy of Management Annals*, 14(2), 627–660.

Guszca, J., Rahwan, I., Bible, W., Cebrian, M. & Katyal, V. (2018). Why we need to audit Algorithms. *Harvard Business Review.* 28 November. https://hbr.org/2018/11/why-we-need-to-audit-algorithms, accessed 1 June 2019.

High-Level Expert Group on AI. Ethics Guidelines for Trustworthy AI (2019). https://ec.europa.eu/futurium/en/ai-alliance-consultation, April.

Hosny, A., Parmar, C., Quackenbush, J., Schwartz, L.H., & Aerts, H.J. (2018). Artificial intelligence in radiology. *Nature Reviews Cancer*, 18(8), 500–510.

Mali, B., Bronkhorst-Giesen, C., & den Hengst, M. (2017). *Predictive policing: Lessen voor de toekomst. Een evaluatie van de landelijke pilot.* Horn, Limburg: Politieacademie.

O'Neil, C. (2016). *Weapons of math destruction: How big data increases inequality and threatens democracy.* New York: Crown.

Raisch, S., & Krakowski, S. (2021). Artificial intelligence and management: The automation–augmentation paradox. *Academy of Management Review*, 46(1), 192–210.

Salganik, M.J., Maffeo, L., & Rudin, C. (2020). Prediction, machine learning, and individual lives: An interview with Matthew Salganik. *Harvard Data Science Review.* DOI: 10.1162/99608f92.eecdfa4e.

7. Algorithmic brokers

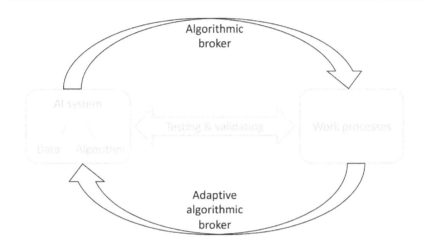

Figure 7.0   Overview of core themes: Chapter 7

7.1   INTRODUCTION

In the previous two chapters, we talked about the fact that developing an artificial inteligence (AI) system requires organizing for data, as in order to train an AI system, data should be created, collected and cleaned. This, however, is not yet a guarantee for successful use in practice. In Chapter 6, we have already highlighted that testing and validating AI systems is necessary before it can be fully deployed in practice. In addition, due to the complex nature of learning algorithms (see Chapter 2), the outcomes are often black-boxed. In other words, users generally cannot understand or see what suggestions or predictions the AI system is based on, which can have negative consequences for how well users trust a system's suggestions. Therefore, it seems vital that the outcomes of AI systems are translated into practice. This 'bridging' or 'translation' is performed by workers inhabiting a new role that we increasingly see emerging in organizations: the so-called 'algorithmic broker'.

Relatively little is known about what happens with the outcomes of AI. This is a relevant issue, however, as a gap often exists between the mathematical knowledge generated by AI and the domain knowledge of the intended users. The fact that an algorithm can predict, by means of calculations, whether or not someone will commit another criminal activity does not mean that judges with their many years of experience will simply adopt this view (Christin, 2017; Christin and Brayne, 2020). Some studies refer to the importance of interpreting outcomes of algorithms (Faraj et al., 2018; Kellogg et al., 2020). For example, Bader and Kaiser (2019) have examined the use of an interface or dashboard, but they do not consider the effect of this on the use of AI. There are also a few studies that refer to 'algorithmic translators' (Henke et al., 2018; Kellogg et al., 2020). However, the question remains what exactly this translation means in practice, in order for it to be facilitated from a management perspective.

In this chapter, we address algorithmic brokering, in which employees are responsible for translating the results of AI for its users (Waardenburg et al., 2020). We highlight the tasks and responsibilities associated with translating the results of AI systems that are incorporated in various forms of algorithmic brokering. We start with 'regular' algorithmic brokering, in which the results of the AI system are translated for users, but no feedback is provided to developers. However, our cases show that 'adaptive' algorithmic brokering is also possible, where feedback to the developers is facilitated, providing guidance for the further development of the AI system (see Figure 7.1).

Our cases also demonstrate that the implementation of algorithmic brokering and the associated tasks and responsibilities entails risks. Accordingly, we discuss how an organization should deal with the implementation and use of algorithmic brokering. We conclude the chapter with a consideration of the challenges related to the implementation of algorithmic brokering.

7.2   ALGORITHMIC BROKERS IN PRACTICE

In this section, we first clarify what algorithmic brokering basically entails: closing the gap between the outcomes generated by the AI system and the user. The police and ABN AMRO demonstrate what this means and why organizations can or should opt for algorithmic brokering. The LUMC and MultiCo are examples of adaptive algorithmic brokering, which includes feedback to the developer. We discuss the added value of such a circular process. The case of the police then closes off with the possible risks of introducing algorithmic brokering, which enables organizations to prepare for this accordingly.

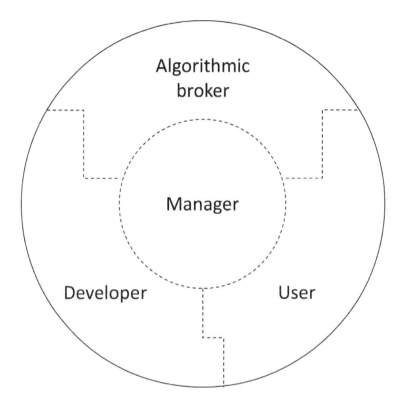

Figure 7.1   Algorithmic broker in context

7.2.1   Regular Algorithmic Brokers

Those who perform the task of algorithmic brokering have the responsibility to make the results of AI systems applicable in practice, but they generally have no influence on the further development of the AI system. The cases in this section illustrate which tasks such 'regular' algorithmic brokering can entail, and who can be appointed for this. At the police, a new role was developed for this purpose, in which contextualizing the relatively raw AI outcomes is the most important work. At ABN AMRO, the decision was made to appoint several end users for the task and to explain the AI system to them, allowing them to support the rest of their colleagues. However, given the fact that the data and the algorithm should not fall into the wrong hands, it is essential that only a very limited number of people are aware of all the details. Thus, for

ABN AMRO's algorithmic broker, knowledge of the system must remain limited.

Police: predictive policing
In Chapter 6, we described one of the main learning points of the Crime Anticipation System (CAS) test phase: how the system is implemented and embedded in everyday operations must be much better organized. An important consequence of this advice was the introduction of the so-called 'intelligence officer' who acts as an algorithmic broker between the outcomes of the AI system, police managers and police officers as the final users. The black-boxed and mathematical nature of CAS ensures that police managers and officers themselves cannot see or understand the motivation behind the results of the AI system. That is why it is extremely important to make the results of the CAS usable in the field.

The role as it is currently performed was created in 2012, along with the initial development of CAS, especially for the purpose of algorithmic bro-kering between increasingly advanced AI systems and police work. This new role is filled by former 'information workers', a position of relatively low status, whose main task is to support police managers and officers in gathering information. Although the information officers have no prior knowledge of data science, nor (necessarily) of police work, because not every information officer has experience 'on the street', their knowledge of police databases ensures that they are the right candidates for the position of intelligence spe-cialist, thus fulfilling the duties and responsibilities of the algorithmic broker.

The direct outcome of the CAS is a map which illustrates – in blocks of 125 m^2 in different colours – at which location the chance of a certain type of crime is highest; and a line graph with blocks of four hours for the corresponding times (see Chapter 4 for an example). To ensure that CAS outputs are used in practice, the project team states that these results should reflect 'what officers [themselves] would say'. This, of course, does not match the map and graph, that still have to be analysed in order to determine where, when and why police action is needed, and what can be done to reduce predicted crime prevalence. The project team therefore gives intelligence officers the task of creating 'ready-to-use' documents by adding contextual information to the results of the AI system. In this way, the results are applicable for police managers and officers. Within the police, this task is referred to as 'enrichment'.

In order to enrich the location and time indications, the intelligence officers make use of the information available in various police databases and general information that anyone could find on the internet. Based on this information, they add more details to the CAS outputs, such as the type of house for which burglary is predicted (for example, 1930s, new construction, student flats). This gives an indication what the reason for burglaries could be, which officers can then anticipate. They also add, for example, which modus operandi is used, or which known suspects often appear at a specified location. Later in this section we provide more insight into the possible risks of enriching CAS outcomes by intelligence officers.

Intelligence officers are thus positioned between the AI system and actual police work. Through their work, they influence how police managers and officers understand and accept the results in their operational work. Although intelligence officers can detect that something does not work, they have no influence on how the system is developed further.

ABN AMRO: money laundering prediction
The development of ABN AMRO's AML system is aimed at supporting the work of analysts by providing better and new alerts regarding the detection of suspicious transactions. Due to the black-boxed nature of the machine learning models, the underlying reasons as to why alerts are issued are often difficult to explain to analysts. However, the analysts do require some basic information about these alerts in order to conduct further investigation. For this purpose, a number of experienced analysts have been appointed to conduct algorithmic brokering and thus support the other analysts in using the AI systems. They form an important link between developers and analysts.

Additionally, the developers have been given the task by the organization to provide the analysts with sufficient guidance in this process. They offer support, for example, by programming a 'translation machine' that can provide information in simple language, allowing the analysts to conduct further investigation into the transactions. This translation machine can, for instance, produce a list of the three top indicators that led to an alert being issued, or the top 20 of the most relevant transactions for an alert. These indicators vary by organization and are not available to the public. The Dutch Secretaries of Justice and Finance have published a general list of indicators. These indicators are thus not directly related to ABN AMRO's AI system, but can give a general impression of what these indicators can entail. This list includes, for example:

- Unusually large cash withdrawals, deposits and cash payments.
- Money exchange transactions of unusually large amounts.
- Transactions above a certain limit, which cannot be explained from the regular business operations of a customer.

The fact that the top indicators are not available is naturally related to the high level of confidentiality of the data and the algorithm used by the bank. For this reason, the exact adjustment and settings of the algorithms are not widely shared (even as they are black-boxed and already difficult to understand).

It will come as no surprise that, for a bank, it is highly essential that such information does not fall into the hands of criminals. As one of the informants explains: 'There is now also a strict separation between what operations [the analyst] does and how the settings and configurations [the outputs of the AI system] are established.'

Additionally, in order to perform the work of an analyst, it is not necessary to fully comprehend the machine learning model. Instead, a lot of attention is paid to explaining and thus enhancing the applicability of the results. Also in the case of ABN AMRO, the analysts who conduct algorithmic brokering do not directly influence the further development of the AI system.

The police and ABN AMRO both provide insights into how companies can deal with the black-boxed nature of AI systems and how algorithmic brokering can make the outputs usable. At the police, the decision is made to create a new role for this. The algorithmic brokers at the police mainly add information to the existing outputs, in order to better match these to the contextual perception of the police managers and officers. As such, they are generally concerned with 'translating', 'interpreting' and 'contextualizing'. In section 7.2.3, we explain how 'correction' and 'adaptation' are added to this. At ABN AMRO, several end users are made responsible for algorithmic brokering between the AI system and work. This is mainly about finding an underlying cause of the alerts, so that the analysts can proceed with their investigation. At ABN AMRO, it is therefore generally about 'translating' (for which a 'translation machine' has also been created by the developers) and 'explaining'. ABN AMRO also provides insight into why an organization can opt for algorithmic brokering without a direct connection with the developers. Given the potential risk of obtaining too much information, the analysts and developers are separated to a certain extent. In the next section, we highlight two cases where the organizations have made the connection between the algorithmic broker and the developer possible for providing feedback.

7.2.2   Adaptive Algorithmic Brokers

Some organizations choose to take a more holistic approach to algorithmic brokering by creating a 'circular' system. Through so-called 'adaptive' algorithmic brokering, the activities related to making the AI outcomes applicable are executed and, additionally, feedback is provided to the developers. This feedback enables developers to adapt AI systems more effectively to the needs of the domain (see Figures 7.2 and 7.3 for the difference between regular and adaptive algorithmic brokering). The cases in this section provide insight into what adaptive brokering entails. In the case of the LUMC, algorithmic brokering is still under development. The case demonstrates how an organization does not have to take the leap right away, but can choose to develop this role in small steps. The case of MultiCo, where adaptive brokering has already been fully deployed, provides insight into the possible tasks and responsibilities of an adaptive algorithmic broker.

Figure 7.2   Algorithmic broker

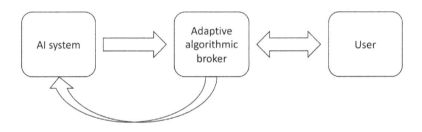

Figure 7.3   Adaptive algorithmic broker

LUMC: predictive tumour modelling
In Chapter 5, we described that the radiology department of the LUMC has chosen to create a new group – the Imaging Services Group (ISG) – with a specific focus on medical image processing, which makes the development and implementation of AI possible. To close the gap between the developers of AI systems and radiologists, the group was launched with eight medical imaging and radiation experts and a technical-medical specialist, equipping the department with the expertise of both clinical and technical aspects of medical image processing.

At the time of writing this book in summer 2020, the ISG had existed for about 18 months, and is therefore still relatively new. The changes are thus far from complete, nor are they institutionalized. Currently, the members of the ISG primarily have a supporting role in the work processes of radiology as an algorithmic broker, because they execute image analysis and reporting for radiologists.

By means of an advisory committee, the Radiology department decides which tasks can be taken over from radiologists by the members of the ISG. To ensure that these tasks meet all conditions for medical care, the ISG develops a protocol for each (image analysis) task together with radiologists. This allows the members of the ISG, as algorithmic brokers, to take over the simpler, image processing and AI-related tasks from the radiologists. In turn, this gives radiologists more time to perform more complex tasks (see Chapter 8 for more details on changes in radiologists' work).

In addition, a standardized reporting format is prepared by the members of the ISG for presenting image analyses. Before the introduction of the ISG, the format of such image analysis reports depended on the radiologists' personal preferences and thus existed in many different formats. Through the use of a standardized format, the results of image analyses are collected in a standard overview which can be converted by the ISG member and shared with different physicians. The advantage of such a standardized format is thus that it makes it easier to share images with various physicians from different specializations. In addition, different reports can be compared with each other more easily, because they are all drawn up in the same way. Follow-up studies are also more standardized and these results can be used more easily for future scientific research, to improve patient care and operational management.

By making the ISG responsible for image processing, the department is thus placed as an algorithmic broker between the AI systems and the radiologists. This allows the ISG to ensure that AI solutions are applied consistently and spread across a larger group of users. Moreover, despite the current more clinical focus, the long-term intention is that the ISG will fulfill algorithmic brokering that is also closely involved in the development, testing and implementation of AI systems. In this way, the members of the ISG, with their knowledge of both the clinical and the technical aspects of image processing, can positively influence the further development of the AI systems so that they match the radiologists' work processes as closely as possible. The ISG has thus been deployed to slowly develop into an adaptive algorithmic broker that affects both the work of the user and the development of AI systems.

MultiCo: predictive people analytics
For MultiCo's human resources (HR) department, the algorithm was developed by an external party. The developers provided the measuring instruments for generating predictions about applicants, while the HR professionals, in collaboration with a specially appointed people analytics (PA) team, acted as algorithmic brokers to make the results applicable for the hiring managers. Although HR professionals are responsible for the recruitment and selection process, hiring managers are in direct contact with applicants after they have successfully completed the AI-based recruitment rounds.

To understand algorithmic brokering properly, it is important to first provide a little more information on the PA team, which fulfils the algorithmic broker function together with the HR professionals. This team was set up by the organization to get the AI project off the ground and further support it. It consists of a PA manager, a new role created for the project, and several data analysts, working from MultiCo's office in India. The PA manager has a background in economics and econometrics and is responsible for bridging knowledge between developers of NeuroYou and HR professionals of MultiCo. The primary responsibility of the PA team's data analysts is to perform specialized analyses and create new visualizations regarding the candidates selected by the AI system. This is done at the request of the HR professionals. We will revisit this subject later on.

The first moment that hiring managers come into contact with applicants is during the group interview. For this, HR professionals do the preparatory work which, currently, mainly consists of interpreting the results of the AI system. More specifically, they first interpret the candidate's match score and decide on the basis of a fixed threshold whether or not the candidate can go through to the next round. Information about the selected candidates is presented to the hiring managers during a briefing prior to the group interview. HR professionals then present a dashboard (a PowerPoint slide) for each candidate with: the candidate's match score in percentage, a word cloud with the most important character traits, and career values of the candidate that emerged from the online games. This is automatically generated by the AI system (see Figures 7.4 and 7.5).

Source: MultiCo.

Figure 7.4   Example of a word cloud of character traits

When the HR professionals initially prepared the briefing for hiring managers, they used automatically generated visualizations. In doing so, however, two problems arose. First of all, the actual meanings of certain properties in the word cloud (for example, the term 'gregariousness') were generally not clear to hiring managers. These so-called psychometric terms are not used internally

Source: MultiCo.

Figure 7.5   Example of a word cloud of career values

in the organization, but fitted the measuring instruments used by the developer. When creating the AI system, the developer was unaware that these terms were likely to be complex and non-intuitive to users. Secondly, it is often unclear to hiring managers whether possessing a certain quality is actually good or bad. For example: is being sensitive a good or bad quality to have as an employee?

In order to eliminate these doubts and ambiguities for hiring managers, and to convey the analytical results more efficiently, the HR professionals asked the PA team to develop tools that simplify the results of the AI system, making them easier to visualize. An example of a new visualization created by the PA team is the spider chart (see Figure 7.6), based on the word cloud mentioned above. This spider chart appeals much more to the imagination of hiring managers, because the applicant's characteristics are not just shown as a word, but are compared with how successful and less successful employees score on these characteristics (by means of a line for the scores of the candidate, and a line for the average scores of the successful and unsuccessful employees in the spider chart). In addition, not all character traits of a candidate are shown in the spider chart. The most important information is prioritized in advance by the HR professionals and the PA team, so managers do not get overwhelmed by an abundance of data.

The joint algorithmic brokering by HR professionals and the PA team goes one step further. HR professionals also help hiring managers to formulate interview questions based on the generated outcomes, which can be posed to the applicants during the group interview. For example, the aforementioned property 'sensitivity' includes the question: 'Have you ever experienced a situation where your emotions got in the way and how did you deal with this?' By linking a question to a score calculated by the AI system, the HR professionals create a format that better reflects the language of hiring managers. In other words, translating the outcomes of the AI system makes it tangible and practical for hiring managers.

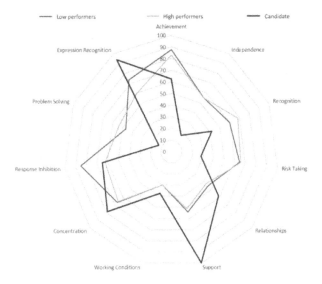

Source: MultiCo.

Figure 7.6   Example of a spider chart of career values

Finally, the work of the PA team and HR professionals does not stop with translating the AI results for hiring managers. In their role as algorithmic broker, they communicate the adjustments they apply to the visualizations to the developers. As a result, the developers make modifications to the AI system, for example, to automatically generate a spider chart. By deploying the HR professionals and the PA team together as an algorithmic broker, MultiCo thus makes adaptive algorithmic brokering possible. The HR professionals are in direct contact with hiring managers, who use the AI system in practice. At the same time, the HR professionals (also after the development phase), through their connection with the PA team, can influence the further development of AI system.

The two cases mentioned above provide insight into the opportunities of a more complex, adaptive algorithmic broker. As the adaptive broker influences the further development of AI systems, it allows it to be adapted to the requirements of its users. The case of the LUMC provides insight into how the hospital takes small steps to organize for such an adaptive broker. This case demonstrates that this role requires organizational adjustments, in order to build it from the ground up. In addition, both the LUMC and MultiCo have opted to organize the adaptive broker in an interdisciplinary manner. The case of MultiCo illustrates how large multinationals – where algorithmic brokering sometimes has to take place between different countries – can organize for an adaptive broker. Of course, there are also risks associated with the responsibilities and expertise that algorithmic brokers develop with respect to AI systems. We will take a closer look at this next.

7.2.3   The Risks of Algorithmic Brokering

In the previous two subsections, we discussed the responsibility of algorithmic brokering as an intervention to bridge the gap between the knowledge generated by AI systems and the domain knowledge of users. The results of AI systems are often abstract and the black-boxed nature of these systems makes it difficult to interpret them. In this subsection, we explain that the tasks of algorithmic brokers are certainly not simple and should not be considered to be a 'holy grail'. The tasks performed by algorithmic brokers can guarantee the applicability of AI systems, but it is important that their work process is carefully managed. When the organization loses sight of how algorithmic brokers operate – in other words, which actions are performed to make the AI system relevant to the domain in which it is used – the chance exists that algorithmic brokers will filter and interpret in such a way that they make the outcomes of AI systems increasingly subjective. We use the case of the police to outline these risks.

Police: predictive policing
With the introduction of CAS, the intelligence officers took a two-day course, in which the basic principles of the AI system were explained and where the work process that is expected of them was discussed (focused on enriching outputs, as we discussed in section 7.2.1). However, the course appears to be far from sufficient for the intelligence officers to conduct their work properly. For example, it has not been further explained what (which variables) the CAS algorithm actually consists of. Understanding the algorithm, however, appears to be fundamental to how CAS outputs are translated by intelligence officers.

The work of the intelligence officers in terms of CAS mainly consists of creating an overview of the CAS predictions and adding extra information. This overview is shared with police managers and later with police officers. To this day, police managers and police officers do not look at the direct CAS outputs, but only at the translated, interpreted list prepared for them by the intelligence officers.

When CAS was first introduced, the intelligence officers added all CAS predictions to their overview. However, the longer the intelligence officers worked with the CAS outputs, the more they started to doubt the outcomes of the AI system. The intelligence officers faced more and more ambivalent predictions; for example, predicted car burglary at locations where cars cannot or are not allowed to enter. Statistically, such a prediction may be correct, but in practice it is of little use to a police team. As a result, instead of copying and pasting all predictions and simply enriching them, predictions are increasingly labelled as incorrect by the intelligence officers and then removed from the overview.

The intervention by the intelligence officers means that information is not so much translated, allowing it to become meaningful for the police officers, but rather that the information from the AI system is curated by them.[1] The curated document contains only that information which is deemed important or relevant by the intelligence officers. Because police managers and officers never look at the actual outcomes of the AI system, but completely trust what is handed to them by the intelligence officers, they are not aware of the subjective and limited nature of this document. In contrast, they even continue to regard this curated document as the outcome of the AI system.

Work processes are now being developed at various Dutch police stations where intelligence officers present the curated results to police managers once a week during a management meeting. In doing so, they advise management concerning where and when police officers should be deployed. Among police management, there is increasing confidence in the validity of the insights of an AI system compared to the individual knowledge of the employee, which is why the advice of the intelligence officers is almost literally taken over by the managers and converted into so-called work assignments (such as surveillance in a particular neighbourhood in a particular time frame). Such work assignments have to be performed by police officers when they are not dealing with an emergency. The problem with the (invisibly) curated advice from intelligence officers, however, is that this concerns only a small part of what is actually predicted by the AI system and, on top of this, is a subjectively constructed document. Police managers and officers will never know what (else) they could have foreseen.

This case shows what can happen if organizations lose sight of the tasks performed by the algorithmic broker. When the users do not develop any further knowledge about the AI system, they depend on the algorithmic broker, which makes it easy to miss what actually happens with the outcomes of the AI system. Implementing an algorithmic broker does not mean that it has to take over all AI-related tasks from users, but that it must support the user in understanding and using AI systems. In this way, the users themselves can continue to critically examine what the results actually mean within their work domain.

7.3 THE CHALLENGES OF ALGORITHMIC BROKERING

In section 7.2, we analysed examples of the implementation of algorithmic brokering as an intervention to bridge the gap between the knowledge generated by AI systems and the domain knowledge of users. We discussed what an algorithmic broker essentially entails and the more extensive version: adaptive algorithmic brokering, which includes feedback to the developer. We concluded with the risks of algorithmic brokering. In this section, we take this a step further. Building on the cases and existing (mainstream) scientific literature, we identify three challenges that need to be taken into account when implementing and embedding algorithmic brokering in the organization:

1. How do you ensure 'objective' algorithmic brokering?
2. Who can perform algorithmic brokering and within what time frame?
3. How do you ensure circularity in algorithmic brokering?

7.3.1   How Do You Ensure 'Objective' Algorithmic Brokering?

One of the promises and goals of the development and use of AI systems is that, because they can generate their own rules and connections based on large amounts of data, they can generate more objective[2] outcomes than humans can (Davenport and Kirby, 2016; Mayer-Schönberger and Cukier, 2013). However, in this chapter, we have demonstrated that when algorithmic brokering is used to close the gap between AI system and humans, this can affect the objectivity of the results. After all, the human decisions involved in algorithmic brokering are susceptible to subjectivity as a result of short-term memory, personal preferences, cultural backgrounds, and so on. When there is no contact with the developer during algorithmic brokering, a one-sided translation of the results of the AI system takes place. For an organization, it is important to have a good overview of this, since the end user can act differently based on subjectively constructed information. It is thus essential for an organization to consider which tasks, responsibilities and freedoms apply to this role when implementing an AI system with the associated algorithmic brokering.

As the cases in section 7.2 demonstrate, algorithmic brokering mainly arises from the need to make the black-boxed AI systems explainable and thus usable. In Chapter 3, we have already discussed the term 'responsible AI'. In this context, 'explainability' of the technical aspects is becoming increasingly important, because this is expected to lead to transparent and reliable AI systems (Doran et al., 2017; Gunning, 2017; Santiago and Escrig, 2017). As a result, there is an increasing focus on creating technical applications that make complex learning algorithms explainable and interpretable (Hafermalz and Huysman, 2019). An example of such a technical application is the translation machine created by the developers at ABN AMRO. However, connecting AI systems to work processes does not only depend on the technical explainability of their variables and underlying reasoning; it is also important that the results are placed in the correct context, something for which technical applications are not suitable and for which the human contribution of algorithmic brokering is therefore desired.

However, this contextualizing can result in the further black-boxing of the AI system. As the algorithmic broker provides (interpreted) outputs on a silver platter to the user, users no longer have to think about whether an AI suggestion actually fits within their work processes. Despite the fact that this is highly problematic within the organizational context – because management decisions are then made based on unknown and often subjectively constructed information – the work of algorithmic brokers has received little attention in organizations. The challenge is to find a way to put the results of AI systems in context, without losing their objective nature. Establishing a clear distinction in the presentation to users between the AI-based outcomes and the added contextual information is an important first step that invites critical reflection on the part of the user.

7.3.2 Who Can Perform Algorithmic Brokering and Within What Time Frame?

Although the importance of algorithmic brokering was not recognized for a long time, it is slowly being referred to in the literature (Henke et al., 2018; Kellogg et al., 2020; Waardenburg et al., 2018, 2020). Regardless of the fact that different names are used for this role – from 'algorithmic brokers' (Kellogg et al., 2020; Waardenburg et al., 2020) to 'translators' (Henke et al., 2018) – it always comes down to bridging the gap between the developers, the AI system and its users.

Implementing the algorithmic broker is not an easy process. As the cases in section 7.2 have shown, the introduction of algorithmic brokering requires attention to the development of new tasks and skills. For organizations, implementing and embedding the algorithmic broker therefore takes a lot of time and effort. In addition, for every organization, the question is whether algorithmic brokering should be used until the teething problems have been removed from the system, or whether algorithmic brokering will be necessary on a structural basis for the use of AI. For organizations, an important challenge lies in determining whether the algorithmic broker is used as a temporary solution or as a permanent part of the use of AI systems.

To determine whether the algorithmic broker is required on a temporary or permanent basis, it is important to look at the knowledge and digital skills of the users and whether the organization does (or is planning to do) something about this; for example, by offering training courses in which users can develop their AI-related knowledge. If the organization is committed to training users, the algorithmic broker can be deployed as a temporary solution, until the users themselves have gained sufficient knowledge to interpret the results of AI systems.

Furthermore, it is important to know whether the results of the AI system need to be fully translated or interpreted, or whether users should only be supported in the AI-related administrative tasks. Translation and interpretation require more than mere knowledge of the AI system, calling for new skills that are often beyond the reach or responsibility of users. Consider, for example, the case of the police, where the initial results of the AI system need to be fully enriched.

Whether algorithmic brokering is temporary or permanent is thus largely determined by whether an organization is committed to further training the users and whether the users can take on the necessary tasks (see Figure 7.7 for a schematic overview of the possibilities for the temporary versus the permanent algorithmic broker function).

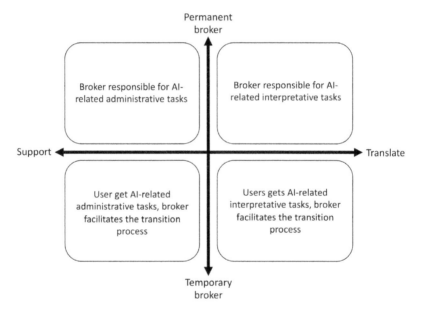

Figure 7.7   Temporary versus permanent algorithmic brokers

If temporary algorithmic brokers bridge a lack of knowledge and digital skills until the users have been retrained, this poses a challenge to organizations as to who should perform this temporary role. ABN AMRO, as described in section 7.2, opted to tackle this step by step, through training and deploying some of the users, who could then be deployed to provide further training to the rest of the users. Another solution could be to attract consultants to fulfil the temporary algorithmic broker role. For consultants, the gap between the outcomes of AI systems and the knowledge of users could be a business opportunity. The question is whether we should welcome this, because detailed domain knowledge is necessary to perform algorithmic brokering. As shown in the cases in section 7.2, it is not merely about standardized tasks, but also about understanding the work processes and the corporate culture and context (as, for example, selecting candidates at MultiCo has shown). In addition, there is a chance that, if the tasks turn out to deviate too much from the daily work of the users, the temporary nature will eventually transform into permanent algorithmic brokering, whereby the organization would have to start from scratch.

Furthermore, especially those who fulfil permanent algorithmic broker roles committed to translating and interpreting the results generated by AI systems must be all-rounders. Particularly, when this concerns an adaptive algorithmic broker function (see section 7.2.3), both technical knowledge of AI systems (the algorithmic broker and the developers must be able to 'talk' with each other) as well as detailed domain knowledge (because algorithmic brokering must make the outcomes of the AI system relevant and usable within the work processes) is necessary. Making permanent algorithmic brokering a central part of organizations calls for individuals who possess both aspects. For the coming years, it will be a challenge to equip people for this as good as possible.

7.3.3 How Do You Ensure Circularity in Algorithmic Brokering?

In the cases discussed in section 7.2.2, we demonstrated that an adaptive version of algorithmic brokering exists. This involves the translation of the AI system to the users, as well as the translation of the practice to the developers. Although this seems to come close to technology development focused on joint optimization, adaptive brokering differs in two areas. First of all, the developers are not part of an interdisciplinary team, but are informed by them. Secondly, even after the development of the AI system, adaptive brokering often maintains a central role in the organization to enable the use of the AI system. The challenge therefore lies in creating a stable, permanent algorithmic broker.

An important challenge in organizing adaptive algorithmic brokering as a permanent part of the organization is to maintain circularity. What an organization must guard against is that there is a chance that the user will transfer the responsibilities for digital skills and knowledge to the (adaptive) broker, with the result that developers and the users remain separated from each other. As a result, the development of the social skills and domain knowledge of developers (see Chapter 4) and the digital skills and technical knowledge of users remains limited.

Finally, not surprisingly, the literature on AI pays a lot of attention to machine learning. Little attention is paid to the possibility of organizational learning in which the adaptive algorithmic broker can play an important role. Adaptive brokers can offer support in translating the results of AI systems into what is needed in practice. They can see what is (not) going well and provide feedback on this to the developers who can subsequently adapt the AI system to this. This is also known as single loop learning (Argyris and Schön, 1997). If the adaptive algorithmic broker also remains sufficiently independent from both the developers and the domain, it can also help the organization to reflect on questions such as:

* Do we actually want an AI system?
* Which issues does it currently fix?
* Are these actual issues?
* What are the possibilities of getting outside the established frameworks with AI?

In addition, adaptive brokers can encourage organizations to reflect on current assumptions with regard to work by, for example, making certain established assumptions visible in the translation of results of AI systems. This can lead to further innovation and change in work processes, which is also referred to as double loop learning (Argyris and Schön, 1997). The challenge is to continue to critically evaluate the work of algorithmic brokers and also to give them an independent role to be better able to support organizations. Double loop learning not only points to responsibilities in bridging the gap between developer and users, but also to changes in work and organization, which we will discuss in more detail in Chapter 8.

7.4   SUMMARY

In this chapter, we have discussed algorithmic brokers, who are responsible for bridging the gap between the knowledge generated by AI systems and the domain knowledge of users. We described different versions of algorithmic brokering: from merely translating AI results for the user, to an adaptive broker that also influences the further development of the AI system. Additionally, we discussed the risks of deploying an algorithmic broker, namely that developers and users subsequently no longer consider it necessary to further develop their knowledge of, respectively, the domain and the technology. If an organization does not pay attention to this, the good intentions of algorithmic brokering can ultimately have harmful impacts and leave both the developer and the user in the dark. We concluded the chapter by stating that working with an adaptive algorithmic broker can support not only machine learning but also organizational learning. In the next chapter, we will take a closer look at organizational learning by unpacking how the implementation and use of AI systems can change work.

BOX 7.1   KEY TAKEAWAYS

- Algorithmic brokers can support in bridging the gap between developers, the AI system and users.
- Insight into work processes is crucial to properly perform algorithmic brokering.
- Depending on the users' further training, algorithmic brokering is done temporarily or permanently.
- Algorithmic brokers can support users in AI-related activities, or translate and explain results of AI systems to users.

NOTES

1. With the word 'curate' we base ourselves on the work of curators, whose work consists of mastering the subject under discussion – for example, through careful work with sources and validating them – allowing them to put together a proper exhibition (Teather, 1990; Waardenburg et al., 2020).
2. We use the term 'objectivity' with some hesitation, as we agree with many current scholars that AI systems are actually never fully objective, since they always include the decisions of, for example, the developers.

REFERENCES

Argyris, C., & Schön, D.A. (1997). Organizational learning: A theory of action perspective. *Reis, 77/78*, 345–348.

Bader, V., & Kaiser, S. (2019). Algorithmic decision-making? The user interface and its role for human involvement in decisions supported by artificial intelligence. *Organization, 26*(5), 655–672.

Christin, A. (2017). Algorithms in practice: Comparing web journalism and criminal justice. *Big Data and Society, 4*(2), 1–14. DOI: 10.1093/socpro/spaa004.

Christin, A., & Brayne, S. (2020). Technologies of crime prediction: The reception of algorithms in policing and criminal courts. *Social Problems*, 1–17. 7 doi: 10.1093/socpro/spaa004.

Davenport, T.H., & Kirby, J. (2016). *Only humans need apply: Winners and losers in the age of smart machines*. New York: Harper Business.

Doran, D., Schulz, S., & Besold, T.R. (2017). What does explainable AI really mean? A new conceptualization of perspectives. *arXiv preprint arXiv:1710.00794.*

Faraj, S., Pachidi, S., & Sayegh, K. (2018). Working and organizing in the age of the learning algorithm. *Information and Organization, 28*(1), 62–70.

Gunning, D. (2017). Explainable artificial intelligence (XAI): Defense advanced research projects agency. https://www.darpa.mil/program/explainable-artificial -intelligence.

Hafermalz, E., & Huysman, M.H. (2019). Please explain: Looking under the hood of explainable AI. Paper presented at PROS 2019, Understanding the Dynamics of Work, Innovation, and Collective Action, Crete.

Henke, N., Levine, J., & McInerney, P. (2018). You don't have to be a data scientist to fill this must-have analytics role. *Harvard Business Review.* https://hbr.org/2018/02/you-dont-have-to-be-a-data-scientist-to-fill-this-must-have-analytics-role.

Kellogg, K.C., Valentine, M.A., & Christin, A. (2020). Algorithms at work: The new contested terrain of control. *Academy of Management Annals, 14*(1), 366–410.

Mayer-Schönberger, V., & Cukier, K. (2013). *Big Data: A revolution that will transform how we live, work, and think.* New York: Houghton Mifflin Harcourt.

Santiago, D., & Escrig, T. (2017). Why explainable AI must be central to responsible AI: Accenture. https://www.accenture.com/us-en/blogs/blogs-why-explainable-ai -must-central-responsible-ai.

Teather, J.L. (1990). The museum keepers: The museums association and the growth of museum professionalism. *Museum Management and Curatorship, 9*(1), 25–41.

Waardenburg, L., Sergeeva, A., & Huysman, M. (2018). Hotspots and blind spots. In *Working Conference on Information Systems and Organizations* (pp. 96–109). Cham: Springer.

Waardenburg, L., Sergeeva, A., & Huysman, M. (2020). Filling the void: How occupational authority emerges from curating learning algorithms. In *Academy of Management Proceedings.* Academy of Management Briarcliff Manor, New York 10510.

8.   Changing work

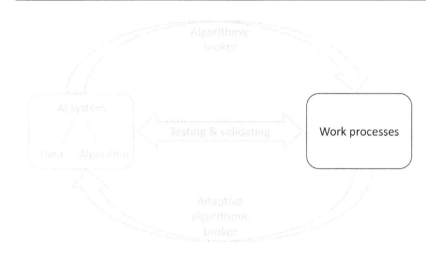

Figure 8.0   *Overview of core themes: Chapter 8*

8.1   INTRODUCTION

In the previous three chapters, we focused on three artificial intelligence (AI)-related areas that organizations and their management should specifically take into account when implementing AI. The question remains: What, in a broad sense, happens to work once AI has been implemented? Reflecting on this question is necessary before implementing AI, because good preparation requires anticipating changes.

Much has been written about the negative consequences of AI, and especially its ability to take over jobs (see Chapter 3). Where previously mainly administrative tasks were automated, now knowledge-intensive professional tasks – such as diagnosing tumours, selecting candidates and predicting consumer behaviour – are next in line. This means that the many years of experience gained by higher-educated professionals, both during their education and during their professional career, can be (partially) taken over by AI systems.

At least, this is what the media has led us to believe for a long time (Huysman, 2020; Willcocks, 2020).

Fortunately, expectations regarding the role of AI at work have become more nuanced over time. First of all, it has become clear that jobs should not be used as a unit of analysis, which was how Frey and Osborne (2013) initially approached the future of work. In their leading Oxford study, they predicted that 47 per cent of current jobs would be lost as a result of robotization and AI (Frey and Osborne, 2017).[1] However, later studies do not use jobs but tasks as a unit of analysis. These studies present much less negative results (e.g., Felten et al., 2018; Forrester Research, 2017; OECD, 2016). The Organisation for Economic Co-operation and Development (OECD, 2016) study, for instance, analysed that only 9 per cent (instead of 47 per cent) of jobs may be lost to automation. Other studies also demonstrate that, in addition, many new jobs are emerging, such as positions related to organizing for data (see Chapter 5), AI auditors (see Chapter 6), algorithmic brokers (see Chapter 7), as well as jobs that we currently cannot even imagine.

As in previous chapters, we take a sociotechnical approach and examine what happens in organizations when AI actually reaches the workplace. As we described in Chapter 3, little is known about the actual impact of AI systems on our work. Most studies on changes in and the future of work have a quantitative approach, looking at how many jobs are being lost and added in numbers. In the field of qualitative research – looking at how work itself changes – knowledge is still very limited (see Figure 8.1 for a schematic overview of the different approaches to the effect of AI on work).

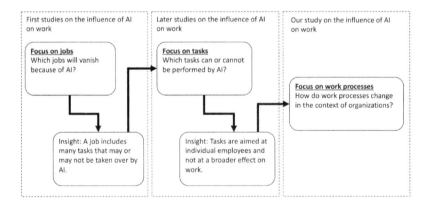

Figure 8.1   Overview of change in focus regarding AI and work

Based on our cases we first clarify that, in many instances, AI systems automate only parts of the work. The tasks that are left to people, such as emotional work and complex and specialized work, are not as easily automated. We discuss how this shift can be observed in different areas of work. When certain tasks are automated with the use of AI, this can naturally also have consequences for the control and responsibilities of organizations and employees. After all, who is responsible for decisions taken by AI, and what does this mean for the execution of work? We will subsequently discuss how changes to work can be properly supported, so that resistance, workaround or unnecessary job losses are prevented. We conclude this chapter with a consideration of the challenges related to changes to work.

8.2   CHANGES TO WORK IN PRACTICE

In this section, CB and the LUMC show that AI can take over certain tasks, yet emotional or complex, specialized tasks remain for humans to perform. MultiCo and the police highlight the changes in control and responsibility that accompany the implementation of AI. Lastly, we return to KLM and CB which offer examples of how these organizations have made changes to work possible.

8.2.1   Augmenting Work

In the introduction, we briefly mentioned the existing fear of AI systems taking over work and making many jobs obsolete. The more optimistic among us state that AI will actually enable people to conduct less repetitive work and have more time for 'more fun' tasks. The more nuanced view is that AI can and will take over only parts of the work or tasks, which still leaves a lot of work for humans to perform (Brynjolfsson and McAfee, 2014). Nevertheless, it is obvious that there will be changes to work if parts of it are taken over by AI systems. In what follows, based on CB and the LUMC, we discuss which consequences are currently visible. For the helpdesk employees of CB the more routine tasks are automated, which leaves mainly the emotional work to the employees. At the LUMC, AI ensures that radiologists can increasingly organize their work around more complex tasks such as multidisciplinary diagnostics.

CB: helpdesk chatbot
For many customers of the various departments of the organization, the customer service chatbot CeeBee is the first point of contact. Despite this active role, however, the chatbot has been implemented as a 'complementary tool' for customer support. Although the impression often exists that the work of

the helpdesk employee is being taken over by the chatbots, CB does not intend to replace the employees with its AI system. The main reason for this is the human touch, that can only be offered to the customer by an actual person (for the time being).

CB chooses not to put the chatbot in direct connection with helpdesk employees. Instead, the chatbot and the employees are considered as two separate communication flows within the organization. Those who are in direct contact with the chatbot are CB's customers. When a customer requests support via the website, they are given the choice between: WhatsApp, the CB App or live chat. Whatever they decide, the customer always starts the conversation with the CeeBee chatbot. When the question turns out to be too complex, the customer is forwarded to a human helpdesk employee.

Because the chatbot can take over the relatively simple questions, the tasks and responsibilities of the helpdesk employee change. Customers now mainly seek direct contact with helpdesk employees when the matters they want to discuss are sensitive or complex. As a result, the helpdesk employees have become increasingly convinced that the chatbot is not taking over their job, and is actually particularly useful for the more practical, straightforward matters, for example, answering a question regarding change of address details. The helpdesk employees believe their value and responsibilities remain in the 'emotional component' of the work; for example, handling a question about death benefits. Due to their many years of experience with a large number of questions, customers and complex, emotional situations, the strength of the helpdesk employees of CB is that they are well attuned to contact with the customer. They can provide current information and emotional support for a wide range of topics.

However, the use of the chatbot also has consequences for the extent to which the helpdesk employees can offer this emotional component to customers. Since the introduction of the chatbot, helpdesk employees have to conduct their interactions solely by means of online chats, whereas this was previously often done by telephone. Using online chats for customer interaction is important, because this data can be used for training the AI system. Yet, the helpdesk employees do not consider online chats to be a suitable medium for handling complex or emotional matters, and still prefer the telephone. A phone conversation, where they can hear the customer's tone of voice, gives them the opportunity to sympathize with the customer, and that is precisely what the helpdesk employees believe is necessary for the emotional component of their work. We describe how the helpdesk employees and the organization deal with the difference between chatbot and human communication in section 8.2.3.

LUMC: predictive tumour modelling

Due to the extent to which the work of the radiologist has been digitized, it is increasingly being suggested that the work of a radiologist will no longer exist in five to ten years. We want to use the case of the LUMC to provide a different perspective. We do this partly on the basis of the developments observable at the LUMC, and partly on the basis of what radiologists have stated in a broader sense regarding the changes they observe within their profession.

The amendments to the radiologist profession can be summarized in two general points. Firstly, with the help of AI systems, a new dimension can be added to diagnostics, for example by detecting invisible abnormalities and by combining different types of diagnostic information. AI systems therefore help radiologists to create an even more comprehensive, complex or more detailed diagnosis, and in this way, to offer better medical care. Secondly, AI systems can help by taking over some parts of the work – especially routine tasks – from the radiologist. This allows the radiologist to 'return to the work of a physician' (which radiologists are essentially) as they can spend more time on diagnostics. As one radiologist explains:

> [I]f we [radiologists] want AI systems to help us, we will also have to spend more time being more of a physician. And being a physician means talking to patients, to other physicians, discussing various diagnoses. And then we can leave the execution of calculations and the more repetitive tasks to AI systems. But then you [as an organization] must allow radiologists to spend more time being a physician.

We are only at the very beginning of the revolution of AI within radiology, but if we are to believe the radiologists, a fundamentally altered 'radiologist 2.0' or even '3.0' will appear in the coming years, with unique expertise in complex diagnoses, as well as the more 'human' aspect of the medical profession.

The cases of CB and the LUMC demonstrate that automation can lead to augmentation of work. While automation of work as a result of AI systems is often seen as the opposite of augmenting work, the examples show that both can take place at the same time. As AI systems can be used to automate simple or repetitive tasks, they can affect work in a positive sense, with more challenging tasks such as emotional work (CB) and complex knowledge work such as multidisciplinary diagnostics (the LUMC) remaining. It is therefore important to consider work as consisting of a multitude of tasks and to understand that the introduction of AI does not eliminate all work, but only parts of it. Consequently, it may well be possible that, as a result of AI, work eventually becomes more specialized. In addition to changes in the nature of work, the automation of knowledge-related tasks also affects the division of responsibilities and control in an organization. This is addressed next.

8.2.2   Changing Responsibilities and Control

Due to the large amount of data and the self-learning nature of the algorithms used, it is difficult to trace the basis of decisions and predictions of an AI system. This black-boxed nature of AI systems has consequences for the question: Who holds responsibility and authority over the decisions and outcomes? This change in autonomy can affect the quality of work. After all, if AI systems are going to substitute decisions from experts, how will these experts deal with this? Do they immediately trust these decisions, or does this give a feeling of redundancy, because their carefully accumulated expertise no longer seems to be necessary?

Here MultiCo and the police show how these organizations have tackled the changes in responsibility and control. The example of MultiCo describes how human resources (HR) professionals and hiring managers are aiming to have more input to the development of the AI system, how the developers feel about this, and what this means for the distribution of responsibilities. The case of the police illustrates how the agency of police officers in the use of AI systems is slowly changing.

MultiCo: predictive people analytics
At MultiCo, the use of the AI system to select job candidates involves both HR professionals and hiring managers. Although the HR professionals have been involved in the development of the algorithm from the start (see Chapter 5), its implementation has nevertheless caused surprises. For example, the AI system appears to select candidates who would never have been chosen by the organization: the AI system gives such a candidate the label 'successful', but the candidate is almost immediately rejected by the hiring managers during the interview round.

In response, the HR professionals requested full access and detailed explanations of how the model works from the developers, so they can see how the model chooses whether or not to select candidates. The idea is that, by understanding the exact characteristics and weights that are taken into account, the HR professionals together with the hiring managers can compare where the judgement of the AI system does not match their personal judgement.

However, the developers did not agree to this, on the grounds that the machine learning algorithm becomes abstract and inexplicable once a learning model is produced (see also Chapter 2 for a more technical explanation of machine learning). In the words of one of the developers:

> With the AI system we have now reached a point where we have to make a decision about explainability. We'll keep the explainability up to this: 'these are the tools and we developed them for these reasons. This is the theory we have used for these

reasons and these are the reasons why we use these theories for your organization.' But once a black-boxed model is built, the explainability ends there, because the model does its own thing. Meaning, the results themselves must prove the point.

According to the developers, it is a matter of patience, because you cannot expect an optimal result right away. For this, the AI system must first be fully operational and fed with new data so that it can learn from its mistakes. The developers reassured the HR professionals and hiring managers by guaranteeing that after implementation, the AI system will automatically come up with the right candidates. For this purpose, they must, however, give some agency to the AI system.

The HR professionals and hiring managers agreed with this and placed the responsibility primarily with the developers, but still maintained control over further developments. For this, they use a hybrid form of collaboration (partially realized due to the adaptive algorithmic brokering by the HR professionals; see Chapter 7). Despite the fact that MultiCo has already put the AI system into use, continuous adjustments to both the system and the selection practices of MultiCo are taking place in this hybrid form. This mutual development and modification seem to be an effective way to deal with shifts in responsibility and control.

Police: predictive policing
In Chapter 7, we described the new algorithmic broker role of the intelligence officer, who has become increasingly important for translating the AI system towards the daily work practice of the police. We described how intelligence officers give advice during management meetings regarding the division of labour of police officers. Management implements this advice almost immediately and converts it into so-called AI-based 'work assignments', for instance 'patrol in a certain neighbourhood in a certain time frame'. These work assignments are intended for police officers when they are not dealing with an emergency. With this, their agency regarding when and where to go during patrol has been partially taken over by the AI system.

The fact that police managers started to accept and follow this advice did not happen overnight. For a long time, many police managers and officers were sceptical regarding the possibilities of an AI system for predicting crim, and were therefore unwilling to transfer some of their agency. Therefore, adjustments in the orientation of police work were necessary for the implementation of the AI system. One of these changes entails that the police on the street will have to move from action-oriented responses to increasingly systematic and focused long-term operations. Of course, emergency cases remain a central part of police work, which are nearly impossible to tackle systematically, but actions aimed at long-term problems, such as ongoing riots in a particular neighbourhood, have been given a more long-term orientation.

A second change is that advice to police managers regarding the issues in a certain area is now less often provided by community officers, for this is now increasingly determined by the AI system. A community officer is responsible for a specific neighbourhood and is therefore expected to know more details about that neighborhood than a patrol ('regular') officer. Community officers have therefore always provided police management with information about specific areas. The arrival of the AI system has changed the responsibilities and agency of community officers. Police management considers the AI system as neighbourhood-independent which, according to them, can provide a 'more objective' insight into where the biggest crime-related problems reside. With the arrival of the AI system, management considered the knowledge of the community officer to be 'subjective', while the AI system can 'really demonstrate what is going on'.

In order to facilitate working on the basis of AI predictions, the managers in some police stations decided to fully transfer the responsibility for giving advice from the community police to the AI-based suggestions of intelligence officers. As this decision was made by management, community officers had little control over this.

The cases of MultiCo and the police provide insight into the possible impact of the implementation of AI systems on the agency, control and responsibility of management and employees. The case of MultiCo provides insight into how the lack of explainability of the AI system can make it difficult for users to transfer control and responsibility, and that this requires mutual development. The case of the police demonstrates how the use of AI systems can influence the nature and agency of some work, and what control and responsibility can be taken over by AI in tackling problems. It is to be expected that employees are not always eager for such changes. In what follows, we discuss how employees respond to the implementation of AI systems, and what an organization can do to get employees to participate in the best possible way.

8.2.3   Collective Change

To ensure confidence in the use of AI systems, even when responsibilities and control change, it is important that organizations consider the following question: How can employees be involved in the change process? CB and KLM shine light on this question. With CB, we will discuss how not only the work of the helpdesk employee is changing, but that the expectations of the customer also need to change. KLM has opted for co-creation of the Meals-on-Board System (MOBS), which has resulted in the cooperation of the catering staff. Despite the fact that some of their tasks – to which they were very much committed – have been taken over, the employees are strong supporters of the AI system.

CB: helpdesk chatbot

CB, with the implementation of the chatbot CeeBee, has realized that the promise and idea of AI systems can lead to the wrong expectations among customers. For example, customers who talk to a helpdesk employee on WhatsApp or via instant messaging sometimes think or expect to talk to a chatbot. In live chats to human helpdesk employees, customers regularly ask: 'Are you a robot?'

In the opinion of the helpdesk employees, it is precisely these expectations that ultimately pose a threat to their job. The helpdesk employees regularly try to solve the confusion between whether one is a human or a chatbot with a joke, in order to clarify their role as a human conversation partner. They also appeal more to their soft skills in order to make their empathic ability even more apparent in a chat session.

In addition, the confusion regarding the human input of the helpdesk employee has prompted CB to make changes to CeeBee, allowing customers to make a clearer distinction between the chatbot and an actual person. CeeBee, for example, has been developed as an avatar, making it clear to the customer that they are conversing with a chatbot. The transition to the helpdesk employee is made visible by showing the company logo and the employee's surname once they take over the call. These changes make it immediately clear to customers whether they are talking to a chatbot or a helpdesk employee, so that the latter are less often mistaken for a chatbot and feel more affirmed in their role. Therefore, not only has the work of the helpdesk employees changed, but also the expectations of the customer and the way in which they interpret their conversation with the human or chatbot side of the organization.

KLM: consumption prediction

Developing an AI system for the purpose of consumption production affects several departments at KLM. For example, in Chapter 6, we described that one of the conditions for the use of the AI system from KLM Catering Services (KCS, the user) is that it receives 24/7 support from the information technology (IT) service. For the IT service, this means a change in the work schedule, because staff are now also working night shifts. However, what the project team has focused on most is a change in the work culture of the users of MOBS. As one of the informants says: 'You have made the technology that way, put it bluntly. The human aspect in the adoption of the technology makes it difficult in the long run'.

At KCS, employees have to surrender their trust in their own (often intuition-based) expertise to give in to predictions from the AI system. What makes such a change in work processes so important, and at the same time so difficult, is that the employees of KCS who are responsible for planning the catering are used to having a lot of autonomy. It concerns a job where you have to be able to deal with the pressure and stress just before the departure of a flight, where a lot can go wrong at the last minute, and you have to be able to make the right decisions quickly.

Before the introduction of the AI system, the employees of KCS always made the final choice for the catering on board. They often did this on the basis of gut feeling and the expertise they had built up over time. Although these choices often had to be made under time pressure, the successful outcome of such stressful moments also gave employees autonomy, responsibility and recognition for their work. With the introduction of MOBS this aspect of the work came to an end, because making these choices is no longer necessary, and even undesirable.

To make the transition as smooth as possible, the project team initially ran MOBS parallel to the existing KCS work processes. The employees were thus able to see with their own eyes that the predictions were accurate and reliable, which increased the confidence of the employees in MOBS. After that, of course, a tipping point came after which only MOBS was used. After this tipping point, there was no more room for the earlier work processes in which choices were made based on gut feeling, and actions are merely being derived from predictions of MOBS.

Although you would expect KCS employees to have problems with the transition to AI-based forecasting, this is not the case. There are three reasons for this. First of all, the project team chose to involve users in the development process from the start (see Chapter 6). This so-called co-creation of the AI system made the employees willing to accept MOBS. Secondly, in the phase where MOBS was used in parallel with the existing work processes, the employees were able to see that the predictions were indeed better than the decisions they would make themselves. Thirdly, the work pressure for KCS employees is generally very high – especially just before an aeroplane takes off – and MOBS helps to reduce this work pressure. Therefore, the use of the AI system – in line with what we also described in section 8.2.1 – gives the employees more time to solve complex and often stressful last-minute problems. As one of the informants says: 'The MOBS is not a threat, it is a gift. It offers tranquility in highly dynamic moments'.

Beforehand, to the employees of KCS, changing the work process seemed like a bigger task than developing the AI system, but the time and effort invested in building trust in the AI system has eventually made a smooth transition from 'gut' to 'logic' possible.

Both of the above cases provide insight into what it means for organizations to involve employees in the process of change resulting from the implementation of an AI system. At CB, the work of the helpdesk employees increasingly revolves around the emotional aspects. Therefore, it is important that they are also appreciated for this. Distinction between human and chatbot is very important to them. In addition, the customer also wants to know whether they are talking to a chatbot or an actual person. For this reason, not only is the work of the helpdesk employees changing; the expectations and interpretations on the side of the customer are also changing. KLM's case describes how it chose to involve the users in the development and not immediately overwhelm them with the AI system, but opted for implementation in phases. This increased confidence, causing the users to accept the AI system and make the necessary changes to their work.

8.3   THE CHALLENGES OF CHANGING WORK

In this chapter, we have provided examples of how work changes as a result of the introduction of AI systems. We paid special attention to the qualitative changes to work, including improvements in work as a result of automation, and changes in control and responsibility. Little is known about this subject, even though reports and books have already been written. However, these studies mainly focus on quantitative predictions of the number of jobs that will disappear, and the necessary changes in terms of education and (life-long) training (Frey and Osborne, 2013; Susskind, 2020). Little is still known about the qualitative aspects of changes to work and, in particular, regarding the consequences in practice. It is therefore important to take a critical look at current claims regarding the consequences of AI for work and, above all, to listen to experiences from practice, even if these are still only sporadically available. The cases included in this book help to identify some of the challenges that need to be considered when changing work:

1.   How can we anticipate (indirect) changes to work?
2.   How can we use AI systems to augment work?
3.   How can AI systems be used to learn as an organization?

8.3.1   How Can We Anticipate (Indirect) Changes to Work?

In a response to previously published doom scenarios about AI systems and the future of work (e.g., Frey and Osborne, 2013), studies have shifted their focus from jobs to tasks as a unit of analysis (e.g., Felten et al., 2018; Forrester Research, 2017; OECD, 2016). Although this provides a more positive and realistic picture of the possible consequences of the implementation of AI systems, these studies still provide little insight into how managers can anticipate possible (indirect) changes to work. Based on the cases in this chapter, we demonstrate that when managers want to prepare for such changes, it makes sense to not only look at specific tasks, but to include the entire work process in which these tasks are embedded.

Specific to AI systems and work is that it mainly concerns knowledge work that can be supported by or (potentially) taken over. It is important to consider this, as it means that the consequences of implementing AI systems differ from the previous wave of automation. Unlike the preceding information systems, which focused on administrative processes, AI systems focus on work that requires highly skilled expertise (intelligence), albeit the routine part of that work (for the time being).

When we talk about knowledge work, we are not talking about individual tasks, but about work processes that require collaboration between experts in order to collectively contribute to and share knowledge. Consider a random knowledge work process; for instance, that of a journalist. Although the actual writing of an article is generally done by a journalist, it often depends on the knowledge and understanding of experts of the specific topic to arrive at an article. This also applies to other knowledge-intensive work processes. The expertise that is used as input for knowledge work – to be able to make a decision, for example – is often shared expertise. When AI systems are used for knowledge work, this will therefore not only have consequences for the tasks of the individual knowledge worker, but will also lead to a so-called ripple effect in the work process in which several, often unexpected, tasks change (Baptista et al., 2020; Orlikowski and Scott, 2016).

A simple example of the ripple effect is how police work has changed due to the use of the Crime Anticipation System (CAS). This system has not only influenced how police management decides what knowledge is and is not used, but also requires new tasks from the intelligence officer. In addition, the work of the police officer on the street is changing; not only because an AI system now determines which areas are interesting to patrol, but also because the production of data is becoming increasingly important for these types of systems. A ripple effect of supporting police management with CAS is that police officers are spending more and more time at their computers to report crime.

Anticipating unexpected and indirect effects is not easy, and requires management, among others, to take a sociotechnical perspective on the work processes and to continue to monitor the changes (see Figure 8.1). In other words, because AI systems influence the knowledge that is developed and shared by employees, it is important to maintain a clear view of knowledge work and how this changes as a result of the introduction of these technologies. So, instead of equating work with jobs or considering work as consisting of tasks, the adoption of AI calls for a broader perspective where work is considered as part of the organization's knowledge ecology (Brown and Duguid, 2000).

Changes in one aspect of the work will, due to the collectivity of knowledge, influence other aspects which cannot be predetermined.

Furthermore, most contributions regarding changes to work share the technological-deterministic assumption that an AI system in itself can change work. This is problematic. Although AI systems deliver their own output due to the self-learning element, they are always socially constructed. This means that people do have an influence on whether and how AI changes work (Coeckelbergh, 2020; Glaser et al., 2020; Passi and Sengers, 2020), which makes their impact highly context-dependent. It is important for organizations to realize that this also makes predicting – and anticipating – the effects of AI systems on work even more difficult. It requires more than, for example, deploying consultants on the sidelines. Instead, it calls for a more qualitative approach, focused on personal involvement and familiarity with how knowledge flows and is collectively developed in organizations.

8.3.2   How Can We Use AI Systems to Augment Work?

Scholars pay a lot of attention to how employees may or may not fall victim to AI systems' ability to take over repetitive and routine tasks (e.g., Jussupow et al., 2021; Manyika et al., 2017). A sociotechnical approach, as we use it in this book, provides a different perspective, because it assumes that humans have control over how technology is embedded in work and that it can be adapted by them. An example of radiology is illustrative here. Some computer scientists argue that hospitals 'should stop training radiologists now' (Mukherjee, 2017, p. 12), because algorithms are starting to recognize malignancies with greater accuracy than the radiologists. However, practice shows that radiologists embed AI systems in their work in such a way that they are able to spend more of their valuable time on complex diagnostics (Kim et al., 2021). The work is thus not taken over, but supported or even augmented.

Naturally, we are not the only ones who propagate a nuance regarding the negative consequences of AI systems on (the disappearance of) work. More and more scientists from different disciplines are working on this subject. For example, information technology and computer scientists are increasingly participating in the discussion regarding AI and work, often emphasizing the need to 'keep the human in the loop' in order to retain control over decisions (e.g., Dellermann et al., 2019). Our cases show that by involving users in the development – in other words, through hybrid development – AI systems can actually support and augment work and can become, for example, new assistants, coaches and colleagues.

From a sociotechnical perspective, it is thus likely that AI systems will not so much take over our jobs, but rather change the way we do our work. It is important for organizations to continue to critically evaluate whether AI systems augment work and not unnecessarily over-automate it. As described above, work can be augmented by automating routine processes, leaving more room for more meaningful work, such as personal contact with clients or more intellectually challenging and knowledge-intensive tasks. Thus, it is not a matter of having to choose between automation or augmentation, as is currently widely argued (Daugherty and Wilson, 2018; Davenport and Kirby, 2016), but emphasis has to be placed on collaboration between workers and AI systems in 'hybrid' forms (Gal et al., 2020), and between developers and management for automation to contribute to the augmentation of work (Raisch and Krakowski, 2021).

Consideration will also have to be given to which knowledge, skills or tasks will become more important for employees, and whether further training is required for this. Creativity or empathy may become more important, as is the case with the helpdesk employees of CB; or more specialized knowledge may be required, as in the example of radiology. It is important to uncover these changes, so that the training opportunities and the job profiles can be adapted accordingly.

Increasingly, in response to fears that AI might take over our jobs, the importance of 'meaningful work' is being discussed. Work can become less and less meaningful through the use of AI systems. Consider, for instance, jobs that are constantly being monitored as a result of the use of AI systems (Zuboff, 2019), jobs that are characterized as ghost work (Gray and Suri, 2019), and jobs that are controlled by inscrutable, black-boxed algorithms (Bucher et al., 2021). Think, for example, of journalists who are increasingly assessed by an unknown algorithm or Uber drivers who receive a salary based on a black-boxed algorithm. Increasingly, we see that employees create workarounds as a response to this, such as journalists who mainly focus on clickbait titles that attract as many readers as possible, so that their articles – regardless of their content – will automatically pop up first (Christin, 2017, 2020). When work becomes less meaningful due to the implementation of AI systems, this can remain invisible for a long time. In the long term, this can have a negative effect on both the organization and the employees themselves (Pachidi et al., 2021).

To look beyond doom scenarios regarding AI systems and the future – or lack of future – of work, it is important that organizations focus more on how automation can be used to support or augment work (Pasquale, 2020). However, creating meaningful work also requires a different perspective on what this means in practice. Even when part of the work is augmented, it may well be that the change in its entirety is not perceived as meaningful (for example, when an employee can use their empathic skills more, but at the same time, disproportionate surveillance is conducted). For managers, it is important to realize that determining whether work becomes more meaningful requires insight and monitoring of the entire work process and, from a sociotechnical perspective, determining whether or not AI systems are used to support and augment work.

8.3.3 How Can AI Systems be Used to Learn as an Organization?

Managing AI systems in practice requires more than a risk assessment that can be done prior to implementation. It requires, among other things, the mapping of work processes and associated relationships that exist in knowledge work, to anticipate the possible consequences of AI systems for work. It calls for attention to (additional) training of employees so that they can use the opportunities AI systems offer to support and augment their work. At the same time, it requires managers to constantly monitor work processes in order to determine whether the work is changing as meaningfully as intended.

For managers, the introduction of AI systems therefore implies knowledge of both the work processes in which they are used and their development, to continue to critically reflect on whether they deliver results that benefit the organization. In Chapter 7, we have already discussed how algorithmic brokering can support management in so-called double loop learning. This form of organizational learning (Argyris and Schön, 1997) is of central importance for the organization to develop further in the use of AI systems. As Figure 8.2 shows, organizational learning is a dynamic process. Reflection on and adjustments to the AI system and the underlying assumptions about work are necessary in order to support the work processes as well as possible and to further develop as an organization.

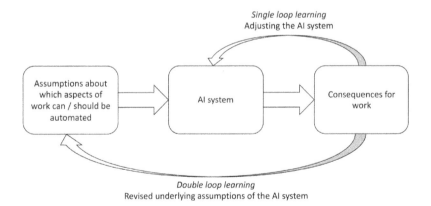

Figure 8.2   Overview of single and double loop learning

The challenge for organizations is to make this constant motion possible. Important here is that managers have knowledge about work processes and AI systems, and that they are also open to critical reflection on the underlying assumptions. For instance, if there is a lot of attention paid within the organization to the consequences of the AI system for work, but no attention is paid to the underlying assumptions regarding which aspects of work can or should be automated (such as the example of MultiCo, where one might also question the assumption that successful employees are good indicators for selecting the right candidates), single loop learning will not be surpassed. This may offer a solution in the short term, but it can create a vicious circle in which the AI system is not used optimally or may eventually even be dismantled.

To continue to learn as an organization together with the AI system, double loop learning is thus preferred, but this also presents the organization with a major challenge, because there is little insight into the assumptions regarding work (Balasubramanian et al., 2020). These assumptions are often implicit, and have been incorporated into the activities concerning data collection and construction or the choices for the decision model. To manage AI systems in practice, it is necessary for managers to pay attention to these assumptions and to continuously reflect not only on the AI system, but also on the underlying principles regarding the work processes. This requires a local presence in both the work processes and the development of the AI system to learn from what is happening in practice.

8.4   SUMMARY

In this chapter, we have considered one of the most pressing questions regarding AI: What will happen to work? We pointed out that we do not merely focus on the doom scenarios – predicting that AI will take over all the work – because automating certain tasks through the use of AI can actually make work more challenging, more creative or more intellectually stimulating. Of course, we are also not blind to the potential dangers, and have explained that the use of AI systems can lead to changes in responsibilities and control. Not surprisingly, the responsibility for some tasks will dissolve with the use of AI. From the cases described in this chapter, involving employees at an early stage of development has emerged as a best practice, in order to ensure that employees get on board, have confidence in the technology, and that responsibilities do not end up in the wrong place. This chapter concluded with the challenges associated with anticipating and organizing for changes to work. We emphasized the importance of observing work processes, and collaboration between experts to anticipate possible changes to work, and showed that managing AI systems in practice is a dynamic process that calls for attention to machine learning and organizational learning. In the next chapter, we discuss our holistic advice for managing this dynamic process.

BOX 8.1   KEY TAKEAWAYS

*   Because AI systems are closely related to knowledge work, which depends on collaboration between knowledge workers, its introduction often leads to unexpected organizational changes. In managing AI systems in practice, there must be room for both machine learning and organizational learning. This requires an understanding of the underlying assumptions regarding which aspects of work can be automated.
*   AI-supported work requires knowledge of how the system functions so that AI outcomes can be properly interpreted and used.
*   The introduction of AI systems in work often entails a change in responsibilities and control, which requires reflection on who makes what choice.

NOTE

1. They looked at data from 2010 describing 702 jobs in the United States, and found that 47 per cent of these jobs had a high automation risk.

REFERENCES

Argyris, C., & Schön, D.A. (1997). Organizational learning: A theory of action perspective. Reis, (77/78), 345–348.
Balasubramanian, N., Ye, Y., & Xu, M. (2020). Substituting human decision-making with machine learning: Implications for organizational learning. *Academy of Management Review*. DOI: 10.5465/amr.2019.0470.
Baptista, J., Stein, M.K., Klein, S., Watson-Manheim, M.B., & Lee, J. (2020). Digital work and organisational transformation: Emergent digital/human work configurations in modern organisations. *Journal of Strategic Information Systems*, 29(2). DOI: 10.1016/j.jsis.2020.101618.
Brown, J.S., & Duguid, P. (2000). *The social life of information*. Boston, MA: Harvard Business School Press.
Brynjolfsson, E., & McAfee, A. (2014). *The second machine age: Work, progress, and prosperity in a time of brilliant technologies*. New York: W.W. Norton & Company.
Bucher, E.L., Schou, P.K., & Waldkirch, M. (2021). Pacifying the algorithm – Anticipatory compliance in the face of algorithmic management in the gig economy. *Organization*. DOI: 10.1177/1350508420961531.

Christin, A. (2017). Algorithms in practice: Comparing web journalism and criminal justice. *Big Data and Society*, *4*(2), 1–14.

Christin, A. (2020). *Metrics at work: Journalism and the contested meaning of algorithms*. Princeton, NJ: Princeton University Press.

Coeckelbergh, M. (2020). *AI Ethics*. Cambridge, MA: MIT Press.

Daugherty, P.R., & Wilson, H.J. (2018). *Human+ machine: Reimagining work in the age of AI*. Boston. MA: Harvard Business Press.

Davenport, T.H., & Kirby, J. (2016). *Only humans need apply: Winners and losers in the age of smart machines*. New York: Harper Business.

Dellermann, D., Ebel, P., Söllner, M., & Leimeister, J.M. (2019). Hybrid intelligence. *Business and Information Systems Engineering*, *61*, 637–643.

Felten, E.W., Raj, M., & Seamans, R. (2018). A method to link advances in Artificial Intelligence to occupational abilities. In *AEA Papers and Proceedings* (Vol. 108, pp. 54–57).

Forrester Research (2017). *The future of jobs, 2027: Working side by side with robots*. New York: Forrester Research.

Frey, C.B., & Osborne, M.A. (2013). The future of employment. How susceptible are jobs to computerisation. http://sep4u.gr/wp-content/uploads/The_Future_of_Employment_ox_2013.pdf.

Frey, C.B., & Osborne, M.A. (2017). The future of employment: how susceptible are jobs to computerisation? *Technological Forecasting and Social Change*, *114*, 254–280.

Gal, U., Jensen, T.B., & Stein, M.-K. (2020). Breaking the vicious cycle of algorithmic management: A virtue ethics approach to people analytics. *Information and Organization*, *30*(2). DOI: 10.1016/j.infoandorg.2020.100301.

Glaser, V.L., Pollock, N., & D'Adderio, L. (2020). The biography of an algorithm: Performing algorithmic technologies in organizations. *Organization Theory*. DOI: 10.1177/26317877211004609.

Gray, M.L., & Suri, S. (2019). *Ghost work: How to stop Silicon Valley from building a new global underclass*. New York: Eamon Dolan Books.

Huysman, M. (2020). Information systems research on artificial intelligence and work: A commentary on 'Robo-Apocalypse cancelled? Reframing the automation and future of work debate'. *Journal of Information Technology*, *35*(4), 307–309.

Jussupow, E., Spohrer, K., Heinzl, A., & Gawlitza, J. (2021). Augmenting medical diagnosis decisions? An investigation into physicians' decision-making process with artificial intelligence. *Information Systems Research*. DOI: 10.1287/isre.2020.0980.

Kim, B., Koopmanschap, I., Mehrizi, M.H.R., Huysman, M., & Ranschaert, E. (2021). How does the radiology community discuss the benefits and limitations of artificial intelligence for their work? A systematic discourse analysis. *European Journal of Radiology*, *136*, 109566.

Manyika, J., Lund, S., Chui, M., Bughin, J., Woetzel, J., et al. (2017). *Jobs lost, jobs gained: Workforce transitions in a time of automation*. McKinsey Global Institute, 1–148.

Mukherjee, S. (2017). AI v. MD. *New Yorker*.

OECD (2016). Automation and independent work in a digital economy. In *OECD Policy Brief on The Future of Work*, Brussels.

Orlikowski, W.J., & Scott, S.V. (2016). *Digital work: A research agenda*. A Research Agenda for Management and Organization Studies. Cheltenham, UK and Northampton, MA, USA: Edward Elgar Publishing.

Pachidi, S., Berends, H., Faraj, S., & Huysman, M. (2021). Make way for the algorithms: Symbolic actions and change in a regime of knowing. *Organization Science*, *32*(1), 18–41.

Pasquale, F. (2020). *New laws of robotics: Defending human expertise in the age of AI.* Cambridge, MA: Belknap Press.

Passi, S., & Sengers, P. (2020). Making data science systems work. *Big Data and Society*, *7*(2), 1–13.

Raisch, S., & Krakowski, S. (2021). Artificial intelligence and management: The automation–augmentation paradox. *Academy of Management Review*, *46*(1), 192–210.

Susskind, D. (2020). *A world without work.* London: Allen Lane.

Willcocks, L. (2020). Robo-Apocalypse cancelled? Reframing the automation and future of work debate. *Journal of Information Technology*, *35*(4), 286–302.

Zuboff, S. (2019). *The age of surveillance capitalism: The fight for a human future at the new frontier of power.* London: Profile Books.

9. How can AI systems be managed wisely?

9.1 INTRODUCTION

A central message of this book is that the various aspects of managing artificial intelligence (AI) systems – that is, organizing for data, testing and validation; the algorithmic broker; and changing work – arise from the unique properties of AI systems: (1) they depend on large amounts of data; (2) their algorithms are self-learning and therefore often black-boxed; and (3) they target knowledge work. This makes an AI system a fundamentally different technology compared with what organizations have previously been confronted with. Therefore, AI systems require new forms of organizing. In the previous chapters, we discussed what it means to manage AI systems using a variety of practical examples. Based on these chapters, we offer four recommendations to make managing AI systems 'WISE' and successful in practice, which requires:

- Work-related insights.
- Interdisciplinary knowledge.
- Sociotechnical change processes.
- Ethical awareness.

Figure 9.1 shows an overview of how the key elements that we have identified are interrelated. We expand on these recommendations in the following sections.

9.2 WISE RECOMMENDATIONS

WISE management of AI requires work-related insights, interdisciplinary knowledge, sociotechnical change processes and ethical awareness. In this section, we discuss these recommendations and their practical implications for management (see Table 9.1).

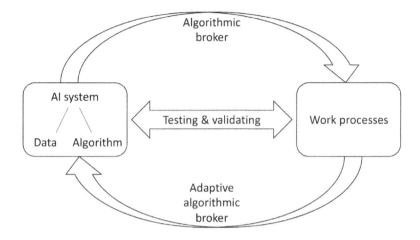

Figure 9.1   Managing AI systems in practice

Table 9.1   Summary of WISE recommendations

W	Work-related insights	Ensure that the AI system is based on work-related insights concerning data, testing and validation, algorithmic brokering, as well as the work processes involved and which are required to change.
I	Interdisciplinary knowledge	Bring different disciplines together (e.g., developers, users, managers, brokers) and provide training where necessary.
S	Sociotechnical change processes	Consider the introduction of AI systems an organizational change process and, vice versa, tailor the technology to the needs in practice.
E	Ethical awareness	Discuss ethical and explainability considerations regarding the AI system and its underlying assumptions.

9.2.1   Work-Related Insights

Including work-related insights means that management choices regarding AI system development and implementation must be made using knowledge of the work context which the technology is aimed to support. The examples in this book have shown that managing AI systems starts with organizing for data. For an AI system to properly connect to the work processes, this data must be related to the organizational context. It is, therefore, crucial to have insight into which data is available in-house, whether the data is representative of the work processes that it should represent, and which assumptions have been made in the data collection or construction.

It is of crucial importance to have a good impression of which organizational or work-related problem is tackled when developing and implementing an AI system. Besides, work-related insights are also needed because the added value of the AI system can only be fully assessed by evaluating its application in the context of the intended work processes. This goes further than just testing the statistical and technical outcomes, as this does not say anything about how outcomes relate to practice (let alone legal or ethical concerns, which we will discuss further below). When organizations bring in external advisers or consultants, who are often assigned to evaluate the technology implementation processes, the organization needs to be willing to provide sufficient work-related insights in the long term. Validating AI systems in practice requires more than just passive observations from the sidelines.

Integrating work-related insights is therefore necessary not only for the manager, but also for the other parties involved, such as auditors, developers and algorithmic brokers. For example, understanding current work processes helps developers to fine tune the AI system to the existing work. This does not mean that all parties involved must necessarily reside within the organization, but the aim is to provide everyone with the necessary organizational- and work-related insights. To facilitate this, it is recommended that an interdisciplinary or even interorganizational team is formed to inform and exchange in-depth work-related insights related to their specific domains.

9.2.2   Interdisciplinary Knowledge

Interdisciplinary knowledge builds on work-related insights and emphasizes the importance of a broad knowledge base that transcends specific domains. To ensure that the organization remains in control of the technology, managing AI systems requires additional training. For example, managers, algorithmic brokers and users require additional technical knowledge. By developing a basic understanding of statistics, workers can value the (potential) contribution of AI systems to work processes, they can critically question the functioning of AI systems, and they can create a more realistic picture of what an AI system can and cannot do. Such knowledge also supports the explainability of AI systems, which will also create more trust in these systems for employees. Finally, providing training (for managers and users) also helps organizations to keep an eye on exactly what kind of knowledge is generated by the AI system. In short: not only the algorithm, but also the people should continue to learn.

Regarding interdisciplinary knowledge, it is often overlooked that developers must also continue to evolve. Considering technical knowledge, we may assume that developers are up to scratch. However, we should not assume that they are knowledgeable about work processes or the organizational context for which they develop the system. Developers are regularly allowed to experiment with data to create AI systems, but the downside of this is that they then often quickly separate themselves from the rest of the organization. This risk is especially clear when developers work for an external organization, but it is still surprisingly common practice for internal developers. Managing AI systems in practice means that developers must be allowed (and preferably obliged) to gain knowledge about the work processes they aim to change; for example, by letting them shadow workers and participate in the workplace for a while.

Additionally, AI system management requires attention not only to knowledge and skills regarding the technology, but also to the further development of 'human' competencies that remain necessary to the AI-supported work processes. If employees should increasingly depend on their empathic or emotional skills, they must also be supported to do so. The same is true for work that becomes more intellectually challenging through the use of AI systems: do employees have sufficient knowledge to perform this work, or does this require further education or training?

The challenge for the WISE management of AI systems is to find a balance between specialist and generalist knowledge, and to pay attention to how this can be integrated to such a level that it can be understood and supported from both sides. Table 9.2 provides an overview of the training we suggest to be required according to type of stakeholder.

9.2.3 Sociotechnical Change Processes

A sociotechnical change process means that both humans and technology change as AI systems are developed, implemented and used. The development or implementation of AI systems (and technology more generally) is often seen as a one-dimensional and linear process that happens separately from the organization. However, the examples in this book have shown that this view is incorrect. Instead, managing AI systems in practice is a sociotechnical change process. An AI system does not just happen to you as a manager – it is not a force that is simply unleashed on the organization – whether it leads to the desired results or not. However intelligent they may be, AI systems cannot (for the time being) develop and implement themselves. For this, they remain dependent on the expertise and actions of different human stakeholders.

The importance of approaching AI system management as a sociotechnical change process becomes apparent when considering that the actual impact of this technology on the workplace is highly dependent on the human choices made in its design. If well organized, this design process focuses on learning and adaptation, and consists of many interactions between the developers,

Table 9.2   Additional training required for each stakeholder type

Type of stakeholder	Developer	Broker	Manager	User
Knowledge and skills required				
Knowledge of data requirements, such as sample selection or the quality or quantity of data		x	x	x
Knowledge of statistics, such as different learning models and their implications		x	x	x
Knowledge of relevant laws, regulations and ethical considerations	x		x	
Knowledge of organizational guidelines			x	
Knowledge of work processes and organizational context	x	(x)		
Translation and interpretation skills		x		(x)
More extensive and specialized knowledge and 'human' skills				x

algorithmic brokers, management and users. Giving meaning to AI systems in the right way therefore requires bringing people and technology together. By undergoing the sociotechnical change process properly, a cycle of adaptation is created where the technology is tailored to the work processes, and the work processes are adapted to the technology. It is also difficult to predict exactly what the technology and work process will ultimately look like, for during this sociotechnical process unexpected consequences or ripple effects can occur. Managers can better anticipate and respond to these effects by being aware and ready to organize for this mutual adjustment process.

Approaching AI system management as a sociotechnical change process is also important to prevent unnecessary loss of expertise. AI systems will not easily be able to replace human knowledge and expertise. As we described in Chapter 8, knowledge work depends on a network of stakeholders; human expertise is therefore more than the knowledge of individual employees. This should not be too easily taken for granted, and it would be a big mistake to regard employees as redundant too quickly when implementing these technologies, as shown in the example of the telecom organization in Chapter 1. Unnecessary dismissal could have been avoided, in this example, if management had carefully considered the entire customer service work process. Then, management would have had a better idea of which activities would continue to require human expertise, such as estimates and assessments based on gut feeling, which likely would have led to the decision to keep the staff.

It is crucial for managers – although mainstream media would have us believe in doom scenarios or the AI 'hype' – not to be afraid of these technologies, but also not to have unlimited confidence in AI systems. Approaching the management of AI systems as a sociotechnical change process prevents these technologies from 'happening to you' and also helps not to turn them into a crystal ball. Viewing AI system development and implementation as a sociotechnical change process provides the space to adapt the technology to the needs of the organization. New work processes must be designed in such a way that they are ready for the introduction of this technology without losing valuable knowledge and expertise. The introduction of AI systems should therefore always be accompanied by an organizational change process.

9.2.4   Ethical Awareness

Ethical awareness concerns the need to discuss ethical considerations and pay attention to the explainability of AI systems and their underlying assumptions. The implementation of AI systems not only affects work processes, but choices regarding, for example, the algorithm can also affect people such as employees and/or customers. AI systems do not have moral compasses, and these considerations must be judged by humans. For example, how data is organized and collected can affect the privacy of employees or customers. As this is unique for every organization, it is not enough to treat legal guidelines, such as the General Data Protection Regulation (GDPR), as checklists. Instead, the necessary time and space must be taken within organizations to critically examine the consequences of choices around data and the models that are used. Related is the question of whether the AI system is prejudiced or biased, or as neutral as was hoped for. It is important as an organization to remain critical during the entire process of development, implementation and use to ensure that no biases develop within the AI system. Organizations must also be willing to step back and determine whether and how to handle biases that develop in their AI systems.

With the growing awareness that AI systems can be biased and that the decisions made by AI systems are often unreproducible, explainability is increasingly considered as the holy grail for ethically acceptable AI systems. Explainable AI is the idea that the black box of algorithmic decision-making must be opened. This helps users to assess whether decisions made by these technologies are fair and correct, and to avoid mistakes, thus increasing the reliability of AI. What management should consider is that the most advanced methods – for example, neural networks – are often the least explainable; while the most explainable methods, such as decision trees, are less accurate. Ethical awareness as part of the WISE management of AI systems requires careful consideration of how advanced versus how explainable an AI system is and should be.

For explanations to be of value, managers also need to determine who the explanation is for. Who is affected by the use of the system? Is the goal accountability, and if so, to whom? Is the goal acceptance of the AI system, and if so, from whom? Or is the goal to learn from the AI system, and if so, by whom? WISE management of AI systems requires active participation and open discussions around both the technical and social aspects involving the use of these technologies.

All of this comes together in the question of who is responsible for the knowledge produced by an AI system. As we have described in this book, incorporating the organizational context is important when making management decisions. The question is whether AI systems will shortly be able to model the complexity of specific organizational contexts. The ethical considerations therefore also include careful attention to what kind of expertise is actually delivered by AI systems to prevent unjustifiable declarations regarding the redundancy of human experts. Managers and organizations must continue to ensure that decisions are ultimately made from the perspective of organizational work processes, and not from blind faith in the results and possibilities of AI systems.

9.3   CLOSING REMARKS

In this book, we have described the different components for the WISE management of AI systems. Table 9.3 combines the key takeaways of the four practice chapters with the four components of WISE.

It is impossible to implement all recommendations in one go. Therefore, we have summarized the consequences of the WISE management of AI in the short, medium and long terms in Figure 9.2. We also recognize that the implementation of AI systems in practice is still in its infancy. We hope that organizations will implement AI in a WISE manner in the coming years.

In this book, we have placed much of the responsibility on the manager. We are convinced that managers, as key decision-makers within organizations, perform an important role and have a lot of responsibility in the implementation and management of AI systems. However, we do not imply that the described responsibilities can or should be performed by one single manager. A wise manager establishes a smart team toward the WISE implementation and management of AI systems.

AI systems offer many opportunities for organizations to fundamentally change work in positive ways. We hope that with this book we have convinced managers to look beyond the AI hype and to consistently question, regardless of the stage of development, implementation, or use: Are we managing the AI systems wisely?

Table 9.3   *Overview of key takeaways and WISE recommendations*

	Organizing for data	Testing and validating	Algorithmic brokers	Changing work
Work-related insights	To develop an AI system that aligns with the intended work processes, developers should sufficiently understand the context-related data.	Managing the testing and validation process requires constant coordination between a team of developers, users and management.	Insight into work processes is crucial to properly perform algorithmic brokering.	In managing AI systems in practice, there must be room for both machine learning and organizational learning. This requires an understanding of the underlying assumptions regarding which aspects of work can be automated.
Interdisciplinary knowledge	Data-related tasks directly affect the AI system. It is therefore important to educate employees about data and statistics.	Testing and validating an AI system requires knowledge of the technical properties of the system, laws and regulations, ethical guidelines, the context of the organization, the work processes and the user.	Depending on the users' further training, algorithmic brokering is done temporarily or permanently.	AI-supported work requires knowledge of how the system functions so that AI outcomes can be properly interpreted and used.

	Organizing for data	Testing and validating	Algorithmic brokers	Changing work
Sociotechnical change processes	Organizing for data involves new data-related tasks. These can be performed by existing employees, or new positions can be created.	A technically well-functioning system does not necessarily provide added value in practice, for this also requires a socially well-functioning system.	Algorithmic brokers can support in bridging the gap between developers, the AI system and users.	Because AI systems are closely related to knowledge work, which depends on collaboration between knowledge workers, its introduction often leads to unexpected organizational changes.
Ethical awareness	Because of the influence of data-related tasks, it is important to handle these tasks with care, approach them ethically, and to take into account the possible consequences of choices from the outset.	Validating AI requires involving the user, to alleviate fear and mistrust.	Algorithmic brokers can support users in AI-related activities, or translate and explain results of AI systems to users.	The introduction of AI systems in work often entails a change in responsibilities and control, which requires reflection on who makes what choice.

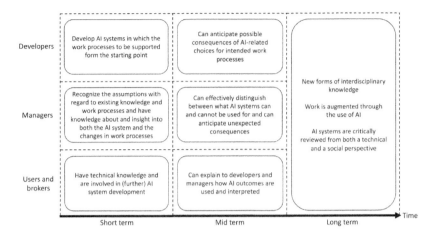

Figure 9.2   Indicators for wisely managing AI systems over time

Index